PickupTrucks

PickupTrucks

John Carroll

SMITHMARK

Acknowledgments

Both author and photographer are indebted to Dale Richardson and Martha Richmond of Greeley, Colorado, U.S.A. and Phil Townend of London, England for their considerable assistance with this book, as well as the numerous owners who allowed their vehicles be photographed.

Photographs

All photographs are by Garry Stuart apart from those on pages 3, 9, 72, 73, 76, 77, 78. 79, 80, 90, 93, 94, 95, 96, 97, 98, 100 which are by John Carroll. The pictures on pages 7, 8, 10, 91, and 101 are from the author's collection.

Page 2: A custom mid-fifties Ford F-100 in the U.S.A.
Page 3: A Toyota Landcruiser 4x4 pickup in Dubai.
RIGHT: The 1955 Chevrolet pickup belonging to Doug
   Brown and Sarah Bradley.
OPPOSITE:
   The same Chevrolet truck appears on this
   album cover reflecting the continuing
   association between pickup trucks and popular
   American culture.

This edition published in 1999 by **SMITHMARK** Publishers, a division of U.S. Media Holdings Inc., 115 West 18th Street, New York, NY 10011.

SMITHMARK books are available for bulk purchase for sales promotion and premium use. For details write or call the manager of special sales, **SMITHMARK** Publishers, 115 West 18th Street, New York, NY 10011.

Produced by Regency House Publishing Limited
3 Mill Lane, Broxbourne, Herts EN10 7AZ, United Kingdom.

ISBN 0-7651-9124-5

Printed in Indonesia

1 0 9 8 7 6 5 4 3 2

Contents

Introduction
THE UBIQUITOUS PICKUP

The pickup has earned a place in American culture as more than mere transport.
It features prominently in country music and advertising and is what the cowboy rides when
he's not on his horse ...

Pickup trucks – those most practical of vehicles – are absolutely everywhere; rusty old beaters and shiny new ones, two-wheel- and four-wheel-drive models, trucks from the eras of classic design as well as the aerodynamic styles of the nineties. So plentiful and hard-worked are they that it is difficult to imagine any economy functioning without them. However, the pickup is more than just a working truck: its appeal has penetrated deep into U.S. culture and it is as American as the cowboy and his horse. Indeed the pickup is the modern day transport of the cowboy, celebrated in the songs of Waylon Jennings, Willie Nelson, Steve Earle, Garth Brooks and many more. Pickups are invaluable: they haul loads, tow loads and are used for camping while the 4x4s are suitable for recreational four-wheeling and a host of other tasks that go towards making the pickup truly indispensable.

When it comes to car production there is great rivalry between those giants of the U.S. motor industry, Ford and Chevrolet. The same applies to the small commercial vehicles that play such an important role in America's economy – pickup

trucks and vans – and any book on the subject has by definition to consider the sheer volume of vehicles manufactured by Ford. The Ford Motor Company has been producing a variety of pickup trucks – more usually referred to simply as 'trucks' – since 1917. Officially that is when Ford began mass-production and it coincided with the massive demand for trucks following U.S. involvement in World War I. There were commercial Fords prior to this date, including a commercial delivery wagon designed by Ford when he was a partner in the Detroit Automobile Company. The main supply of early trucks came through smaller companies who would fabricate a commercial body on a rolling chassis-cab which Ford sold for precisely this purpose. There was also the 1912 commercial roadster body style as Ford began to realize that there might be demand for trucks from the factory. By 1917 the small companies who would build truck bodies onto Ford chassis-cabs had mushroomed and some were carrying out very shoddy work. Ford rightly felt that this could reflect badly on his products so on 27 July 1917 the Ford Motor Company announced a one-ton chassis that would form the basis for a

ABOVE
A Model T Ford truck in the service of the British Army in France during World War I. Military markings can be seen on the truck's hood which is pictured alongside a European express train.

OPPOSITE
A mildly customized 1955 V8 Ford F-100 pickup. It has been lowered, fitted with custom wheels and has had the front bumper removed.

truck programme. This was a chassis stronger than for Ford cars and had a wheelbase which was 2ft (0.60m) longer, had heavier rear suspension and solid tyres on heavy duty wheels. It was tagged the Model TT after the famous car from which it derived.

In 1925 Ford produced the first factory finished truck in North America – the Model T – with a pickup body. Other improvements around this time included improved lubrication systems, pneumatic tyres and a lower steering ratio. The next stage in the development of the Dearborn trucks was when the designs of cars and commercials diverged. This was seen as a mixed blessing due to the reduction of spare parts interchangeability. Chevrolet pulled ahead in 1927 with the best-selling truck in America and it was at that point that the long-running Ford versus Chevrolet rivalry began. Ford soon regained

the advantage when the Model A car and the Model AA truck started to come off production lines in 1928. The AA gave Ford the lead as the effects of the Wall Street Crash were felt, the two companies slugging it out throughout the Great Depression. Chevrolet introduced a straight six so Ford retaliated with a V8 in the Model BB in 1932. In 1933 Ford's cars and trucks diverged once more and this time for keeps. Ford also stayed ahead of Chevrolet in terms of numbers of trucks sold.

Significant changes occurred in 1938 when Ford trucks came with a chassis that conformed to the specifications of the Society of Automotive Engineers' recommendations with better brakes and wheels of larger diameter and there were further improvements: by 1939 Ford trucks came with hydraulic brakes. The same year saw Ford of Canada conscripted into the war effort to build a range of military vehicles. The war halted progress as it did in every walk of life and 1946–48 trucks were essentially only slightly improved pre-war machines. The big news of 1948 was the introduction of the F-Series trucks; these ranged from the half-ton F-1 to the three-ton F-8. The F-Series has, of course, endured until this day.

The F-Series took Ford into the fifties on a very firm footing and it became the nation's number two auto maker, partially as a result of a strike at Chrysler. The F-Series underwent a redesign in 1951 when a new grille was installed. In 1952, two new engines became available, an ohv in-line six and an ohv large capacity V8. The major face-lift was saved for 1953 and Ford's Golden Anniversary – it was the most major redesign in two decades. More significant from the point of view of the truck buyer was that the F-Series was given its modern three-digit designations. The F-1 became the F-100, the F-2 and F-3 became the F-250 and the F-4, slightly downgraded, became the F-350. This may appear straightforward but there were, in fact, 194 models in the Ford truck line-up. This represented a huge investment for the Ford Motor Company and the status quo was maintained until 1956 when Ford was again obliged to act as the result of the introduction, by its arch-rival Chevrolet, of seriously competitive products during 1955. Ford introduced many innovations in an area of vehicle design that was still up-and-coming – that of safety; tubeless tyres, a safety steering-wheel, better door locks and a shatterproof rear-view mirror. Ironically this inexpensive

1962 FORD F-100 STYLESIDE PICKUP

upgrade failed as a sales incentive but ten years later government regulations were destined to impose such measures on the U.S. automotive industry. Innovation in the form of factory 4x4s also came from Ford in the fifties; chassis-cab and pickup 4x4s went on sale in 1959 based on the 118-inch (300-cm) F-100 and F-250 chassis. These trucks were also introduced in response to noises emanating from the Chevy plants concerning its own 4x4.

Another redesign for the F-Series in 1961 included a differently proportioned body wrapped up in new sheetmetal. The wheelbase was lengthened while the front overhang was shortened. Another upgrade followed in 1964 which is when the name Ford appeared pressed into the tailgate and long bed variants of the F-100 and the F-150 seemed aimed at those wishing to carry camper shells. The Bronco appeared in 1966, aimed fairly and squarely at the Jeep, and International Harvester's Scout. The Bronco was the first light utility 4x4 built by Ford since its wartime production of the Willys Jeep. While the Bronco was making the news, changes were being made to the truck line-up which included disc brakes up-front and optional air-conditioning. Ford regained the lead in truck sales for the first time since 1937.

The greatest threat to Ford in the seventies came no longer from Chevrolet but from across the Pacific. Datsun and Toyota were selling their Li'l Hustler and Hilux trucks in huge numbers so Ford sourced what it called the Courier, from Mazda, and badged it as a Ford in order to compete. At the same time the F-Series endured changes, albeit modest ones. It was possible to buy 4x4 variants of both the F-100 and F-250 in 1974. The F-150, a half-ton (508-kg) truck, became available in 1975 and a 4x4 variant of the same pickup followed in 1976. The Bronco was tagged the U-150 in 1978 and was redesigned to utilize many more parts from the F-Series trucks and to change its shape. Sales more than doubled in the following 12 months and took Ford into the eighties, along with F-Series trucks which had once more been redesigned. This was perhaps overdue and covered the whole fleet of F-prefix models. In 1982 the Ford Ranger became a model in its own right rather than a trim package on an Effie and just a year later the Bronco II made its debut and sold at two and a half times its previous rate.

The F-Series survived throughout the eighties with

considerable changes and remained to compete with Chevrolet in the first half of the nineties as Ford's prime trucks. The line-up for this year is comprehensive to say the least. There are three models: the F-150, F-250 and F-350 with maximum gross vehicle weights of 6250lb (2835kg), 8600lb (3900kg) and 11,000lb (4990kg) respectively. The three sizes have increasing payloads of 2145lb (973kg), 3915lb (1776kg) and 5890lb (2672kg) respectively. There are a choice of four body styles: Regular Cab, Super Cab, Crew Cab and Flareside and three trim levels, S, XL and XLT. This represents at least 36 different pickups before the engine options are even considered. There are six different engines ranging from the standard 4.9-litre in-line six through a 5.0-litre V8, a 5.8-litre V8, a 7.3-litre indirect injection diesel V8, a 7.3-litre indirect injection turbo diesel V8 to a 7.5-litre V8. That takes the number of F-Series variants to 216 cubic inches (3540cc) and then there are the various transmissions. There are four possibilities, including both manual and autobox, which increases the number of F-Series variants to 864, competition with Chevrolet dictating that every customer's requirements be amply met. Chevrolet offers similar choices of body styles, engine options and transmissions. If America was not such a big country you could be forgiven for wondering if either of these huge concerns ever make two trucks the same, especially when you remember the numerous colours available from the factory paint shops. New for 1994 was the driver's side airbag in the F-150 and F-250 models. Side-door impact bars are standard across the range and there is a brake shift interlock system on all autobox models. On manual models a clutch of 11 inches (28cm) in diameter replaced the 10-inch fitted previously. The development, of course, goes on; but to fully consider the pickup story it is necessary to go right back to the beginning.

Pickups have been around for a long time, ignoring horse-drawn vehicles, the earliest being cars converted by fitting a load bed. The idea caught on fast and soon manufacturers were offering commercial versions of their vehicles. Henry Ford and others of his era were soon mass-producing pickup trucks and it has progressed from there to the extent that more pickups than new cars are now annually sold in the United States. The practicality of the pickup means that other vehicles have assumed many of their attributes: Broncos, Jeeps and Scouts were given a

OPPOSITE
A promotional illustration prepared by Ford to announce the new models for 1962, in this case the Ford F-100 Styleside pickup. It is described as a styleside to differentiate it from those models fitted with the stepside pickup bed.

ABOVE
Chevrolet 3600 Series hood emblem.

OPPOSITE
A Chevrolet of at least 35 years old when this photograph was taken and still working for a living. It is seen here at Fisherman's Wharf in San Francisco.

load bed and the sport utility was born. While Ford, Chevrolet and GMC are the names that most spring to mind when pickups are mentioned, trucks have been built by Hudson, Plymouth and Studebaker while car-based pickups have included vehicles like the Ranchero and the El Camino. Crew cabs were first introduced in the early sixties and Dodge introduced the extended cab early in the seventies while a couple of decades later the three-door was introduced by Chevrolet. The down-sized and compact trucks appeared in the guise of the Ford Courier and Chevy LUV and are now as much a part of the pickup truck market as the full-size models. In the late nineties Ford F-Series trucks are the best-selling trucks in the United States.

America can rightly be described as the land of the pickup truck, such is the vehicle's versatility and popularity and with four-wheel-drive that versatility is further increased. Willys was among the first to see the advantages that four-wheel-drive would offer to many commercial vehicle users and introduced a range of 4x4 pickups alongside its Jeeps. The trucks differed from Jeeps but the design of their grilles and front wings left no doubt as to which company had designed and manufactured them. The

pickup trucks featured a closed cab with a variety of rear body types, including a stepside, a stakebed and a chassis-cab permitting specialist equipment to be installed on the back. The pickup range was complemented by a line of panel vans and estate cars. The four-wheel-drive models were capable of mounting power take-offs to drive machinery. The first 4x4 truck from Willys rolled off the Toledo, Ohio production line in February 1948 and trucks continued to do so until 1963 with only minor improvements along the way. The grille was slightly altered and a one-piece windshield substituted for the two-piece originally fitted. Until the fifties though, 4x4 pickups from the major U.S. manufacturers were something of a novelty: International Harvester introduced its first 4x4 pickup in 1953 with the R-Series. In late 1955, it being the third largest manufacturer of pickup trucks in the United States, it brought out the S-Series trucks, including the S-120 4x4. There were 13 variations with four different wheelbases, chassis-cabs, stakebeds, and platform trucks. Ford, GMC and Chevrolet also offered 4x4 trucks, usually four-wheel-drive variants of existing trucks; for example, Ford's first contenders for the growing market were the 1956 F-100 and F-250 4x4 models available as pickups and chassis-cabs. In the fifties Dodge built a serious 4x4 working truck based on a military vehicle it had supplied to America's services during World War II. It was known as the Power Wagon and was the undisputed king off the highway in America's backwoods. It was used for logging and oil exploration and on wilderness sites where construction of dams, for example, were in progress. Power Wagons came with a variety of bodies and all were built by Chrysler's Dodge Truck Division and briefly marketed under the De Soto and Fargo names. The Power Wagon spawned a whole range of heavy duty 4x4s, including the Chevrolet and GMC suburbans and crew cabs.

In the mid-sixties the huge American motor manufacturers introduced 4x4 pickups that were available in fleetside and stepside body types and were essentially upgraded versions of their two-wheel-drive models – vehicles such as the Chevrolet K-Models, Ford F-Series and GMC trucks and they spawned a number of sport-utility 4x4s such as the Chevy Blazer, GMC Jimmy, Dodge Ramcharger, Ford Bronco, and International Scout. The Bronco was an early trend-setter and was the first truly mass-marketed 4x4 in the United States. The model was introduced late in 1965 for the 1966 sales year and was available in three versions; open-bodied roadster, sport utility and enclosed wagon. It featured innovative coil-spring suspension and an in-line six-cylinder engine with a V8 as an option. They were fairly basic, options such as power steering and automatic transmission being unavailable until 1973. The Bronco endured in its almost original guise until 1977 when it was replaced by the bigger Bronco which was based on a Ford F-150 pickup chassis and was closer in concept to the Chevy Blazer. The more modern Bronco II is perhaps even closer to the original Bronco concept.

Chevrolet's Blazer was the first of the full-size, big-engined vehicles based on the idea of a shortened 4x4 pickup chassis. It first appeared during the 1969 model year in both six- and eight-cylinder engine types and was designed to use existing and proven Chevy/GMC light truck components that would ensure it gained market-place credibility. The GMC Jimmy appeared in 1970 and was virtually identical to the Chevrolet Blazer apart from certain trim parts. Until 1973, the highest specification Blazer was the CST (Custom Sport Truck) and the Cheyenne specification package was introduced in 1973, a roll bar becoming standard in 1975. All the 4x4 models were leaf-sprung front and rear.

Many believe a pickup to be so useful that, once tried, one will always wish to own one. Some see the humble pickup as the base on which to build a sophisticated cruiser, while others view it as the ideal RV, a recreational vehicle useful for fishing or camping or simply as the most convenient way of collecting the family groceries. In short, there are as many reasons for owning a truck as there are shades of paint. Many remain loyal to their favourites; some favour Fords while others prefer Chevrolets, some like new trucks and others old. My personal preference are the trucks of the late fifties and early sixties but as the specially commissioned photographs in this book illustrate, the tastes of all are evenly represented, across both decades and manufacturers.

There exists a thriving vintage and custom scene among enthusiasts but it is the pickup parked outside a barn or on a Texas highway that encapsulates the myth. That and the roadhouse jukebox which belts out: *'Mamas don't let your babies grow up to be cowboys, to pick on guitars and drive old trucks. Make 'em be lawyers and doctors and such ...'.*

Chapter 1
CHEVROLET

*The Bowtie manufacturer has been making pickup trucks since 1918
and its products attract an immensely loyal following.*

As part of GMC, Chevrolet has manufactured numerous trucks throughout its history. Its first pickups came in 1918 when it made less than 1,000 in both half- and one-ton (1,016-kg) capacities. They were a success, and the following year Chevrolet plants produced in excess of 8,000. In the early twenties the company transplanted a variety of bodies from outside sources onto its chassis-cab trucks and a 1922 Chevrolet three-quarter-ton Model G chassis and cowl, for example, then retailed at $650. This pattern continued throughout the twenties with occasional additions to the range such as an all-steel enclosed cab model in 1925 as well as a panel truck in the same year. By 1928 Chevrolet was becoming a major threat to Ford's dominance of both car and truck markets in the United States and in the last year of the decade produced its half-millionth truck and introduced an in-line six-cylinder engine.

There were rapid progressions throughout the thirties:

OPPOSITE
Chevrolet redesigned its trucks for 1947 and introduced the Advance-Design series. The redesign included the horizontally-barred grille as seen on John Hill's 1951 model and that of Ray Caves (LEFT) from the same year. The latter has a sunshield made in Milwaukee by the Fulton Company.

hydraulic shock-absorbers, vacuum windshield wipers and electric fuel gauges, and external rear-view mirrors all became standard equipment in 1930. Chevrolet acquired a specialist truck body maker – the Martin Parry Corporation – in the same year that led to the company offering a range of half-ton pickups, panel vans and canopy express trucks as factory models. The acquisition of Martin Parry boosted Chevrolet's sales in the light truck market far beyond the 32.7 per cent sales penetration it had already achieved by this time. Throughout the thirties, Chevrolet offered a range of colours, synchromesh transmissions and pushed its trucks hard in fleet sales. All these things contributed to the increase of the company's market share from 33 per cent in 1930 to 50 per cent in 1933, the year Chevrolet produced its millionth truck. Progress was maintained and in 1934 Chevrolet trucks came equipped with hydraulic brakes and cabs were built with one-piece steel roofs.

The trucks of the thirties became more streamlined and were styled in the manner of Chevrolet's passenger cars; indeed, certain models shared the front-end sheetmetal and the range included larger capacity trucks, including three-quarter-ton and one-ton models. By 1933, Chevrolet was selling as many trucks in the half-ton and $1\frac{1}{2}$-ton classes as all the other manufacturers put together. In 1935 the truck range included Model EC and the EA sedan delivery, EB suburban and various EB pickups. For 1936 Chevrolet added a coupé delivery to the range: it was based on the FC-Series of passenger cars. Increases in the range were to such an extent that, in 1939, Chevrolet was offering eight wheelbases and a total of 45 different pickups.

World War II interfered with civilian production as the company turned its attention to the war effort, civilian truck production ending in January 1942. Chevrolet later obtained permission to build a number of trucks to 1942 specifications for high-priority civilian use until civilian trucks were able to roll off the Chevrolet lines in large numbers in 1944. The numerous trucks produced for the Allied cause during World War II meant it was the main supplier to the U.S. Army of $1\frac{1}{2}$-ton 4x4 trucks at that time. These trucks were of a standardized design powered by six-cylinder in-line petrol engines, driving through a four-speed transmission and two-speed transfer case. The chassis was of a steel ladder-type, with leaf-sprung suspension. A steel closed cab

OPPOSITE
A partially restored 1955 Chevrolet truck in Greeley, Colorado. It appears to have been reassembled from parts from more than one truck but now needs little more than a respray to be a neat, straight truck.

LEFT
The grand styling of fifties trucks, such as on this 1957 Chevrolet, closely followed that of automobiles of the same era but was never quite as opulent.

of a conventional design and a cargo rear body and canvas tilt completed the NJ-G-7107 as it was tagged. Chevrolet of Canada also produced trucks for the Allies, including the C30 and the 1311X3.

Numerous variations of the 1942-type trucks were produced from 1944–1945 and in slightly revised forms in 1946. Sales boomed in the post-war years, 260,000 trucks from Chevrolet being sold in 1947. The trucks had been comprehensively redesigned for 1947 – they were described by Chevrolet as the Advance-Design – and now incorporated rear-hinged hoods in a redesigned cab with such innovations as a column shift. The new design was sequentially upgraded with vented windows, new door latches, a redesigned grille, and a new autobox was introduced in 1951. During this period Chevrolet offered half-, three-quarter- and one-ton pickups on 116-, 125.25- and 137-inch (295-, 318-, and 348-cm) wheelbases. In each capacity class they offered pickups in the following configurations, chassis, chassis-cab, pickup, platform and stake. In addition, there were half- and one-ton panel vans and canopy wagons. The three series were designated 3100, 3600 and 3800, increasing with payload and wheelbase. These numerical designations continued for 1948, 1949 and into the 1950s. While the overall appearance of the various models remained the same, there were minor upgrades from year to year as well as increasing numbers of options; in 1950, for example, were included rear-view mirrors, colour combinations, leather seats, chrome radiator grilles, deluxe equipment, double-acting shock-absorbers front and rear, spare wheel and tyre carriers, heavy duty radiators, dual tail-lights, heavy duty rear springs, a school bus chassis, an oil bath aircleaner, heavy duty clutch, four-speed transmission, engine speed governor and numerous tyre options. The series of trucks were redesigned for 1954, two immediately apparent changes being to the grilles and windshields. The grille was changed from its previous series of horizontal bars to a single heavier central bar and a single vertical bar, the name Chevrolet being stamped on the central horizontal. The windshield became a single piece and the interior of the trucks were redesigned with a revised steering-wheel and dash arrangement. Less obvious was the redesigned load bed for pickup variants that was lower at the sides but deeper overall. The three-speed transmission was beefed

up and a Hydra-Matic autobox was an option. The designations 3100, 3600 and 3800 continued although some years earlier the 3700 had been added for the Dubl-Duty models. GMC planned a massive revision of its products for 1955 and included Chevrolet in its plans. The scale of the changes meant that not everything could be ready for 1955 models introduced in the autumn of 1954. The new line of Chevrolet trucks was thus delayed, so for 1955 a marginally upgraded range of 1954 products was released until the new models were ready.

The trucks that were to become legendary were introduced as the redesign from 1955, albeit using the 3100 Series-type designations. The new trucks featured wrap-around windshields, redesigned fenders and truck beds and had the option of a V8 engine. The 3100 was the half-ton commercial while the 3200 was a half-ton on a longer wheelbase; the 3600 was the three-quarter-tonner and the 3800 one-ton. The Dubl-Duty models used 3400, 3500 and 3700 for its various models. The Cameo pickup model appeared as a limited edition and the new design endured with minor upgrades until the restyled model of 1958 was unveiled with its dual headlamps.

ABOVE
The fender emblem of this truck indicates that it is from the 3100 series, the 114-inch (290-cm) wheelbase half-ton model.

OPPOSITE
For many, those of the late fifties are the ultimate classic pickup trucks. It is easy to see why, looking at Phil Townend's beautifully restored red 1957 Chevrolet.

Phil Townend's custom 1957 Chevrolet. The modified truck incorporates subtle changes to avoid detracting from the classic lines of the Chevrolet. Components such as the bed steps (OPPOSITE TOP) and the door mirrors (OPPOSITE BELOW) have been enhanced with chrome.

These pickups rolled off the big lines in Chevrolet's various autoplants around the time that the Americans were testing the first aerial H-bomb on Bikini Atoll and Eisenhower was attempting to enforce racially integrated schools in a place called Little Rock, in Arkansas. One of Chevrolet's 1956 3100 Series models was the half-ton stepside pickup with its 114-inch (290-cm) wheelbase. It was from a range that included panel vans, suburbans and chassis-cabs as well as the stepside pickup. Chevrolet had introduced them in 1955 with what it described as 'taskforce' styling that included new features such as a panoramic windscreen that wrapped around the corners of the cab, a flatter bonnet, wing and roof line as well as the egg-crate grille. The trucks were only slightly upgraded for 1956 and would subsequently be upgraded again for 1957 in a similarly minor way.

The 1958 Apache used the same basic cab as the previous models but featured a redesigned hood, grille and fenders. The fenders incorporated double headlamps and the trim was redesigned. The stepside bed continued although, later in the year, Chevrolet offered what it called the fleetside bed which was more like the smooth sides of the Cameo models but fabricated in steel. A four-wheel-drive transmission was available as an option. The basic styling continued until the new trucks for 1960 were unveiled late in 1959. As was usual, the basic model was upgraded and offered with slightly different options each year. The El Camino rolled out new for 1959 and was something of a hybrid of car and truck with contemporary car front styling and a truck bed between the styled rear fenders. In this year Chevrolet began using the C10–C30 model designations that are still in use today.

The C10 of 1960 was one of a series of 185 trucks made by Chevrolet in 1960. This large number was achieved by the manufacture of 18 different wheelbases among other items such as optional engines and transmissions. The K-prefix models were 4x4 variants of the C-Series. The trucks had been redesigned and changes included a redesigned grille with repositioned headlamps. The fenders, body-sides and hood were redesigned with a sculpted line down both sides of the body. The range included the half-ton Series 1000, the three-quarter-ton commercial and Dubl-Duti Series 2000 models and the one-ton Series 3000 models. Wheelbases available included 104, 115, 127, 133, 135, and 137 inches (264, 292, 323, 338, 343 and 348cm). Engines fitted included an in-line six-cylinder and numerous optional V8s. Minor styling changes took the line into 1961 and a restyled hood took it into 1962. The styling changes were again minor for 1963 but a coil-sprung front suspension arrangement was introduced on 4x2 C-Series trucks.

The 8-millionth truck was produced in 1962 and the El Camino appeared as a mid-size pickup, similar in configuration to the Chevelle automobile. Production was in full swing and a further million trucks had been produced by 1964. The mid-sixties heralded a changing market; the recreational market was growing and worthy of serious consideration by manufacturers. Chevrolet reacted with trucks powered by bigger V8 engines and longer load boxes to facilitate easy installation of demountable camper vans. Production continued at the same rate and by 1966 the 10-millionth truck had left the assembly lines. The trucks were redesigned for 1967 and optional interior packages, including the CS and CST, were offered. Chevrolet felt that this redesign was, 'the most significant cab and sheetmetal styling change' in its history and certainly the trucks acquired a much more modern appearance. They appeared longer and lower and more akin to the styling of the cars of the time as a result of the trend towards pickups for personal transportation and leisure as well as for work vehicles. The trucks were redesigned to slant inwards above the waistline and to have a styling line that defined the wheel-wells and body-sides. The area of glass in the windshield and side windows was increased and the elongated appearance was reflected in the grille that featured two long narrow rectangular panels. The new C10 was offered on two wheelbases in both fleetside and stepside forms and as either a 4x2 truck or a 4x4. The only noticeable change for 1968 was the addition of more brightwork and badging to the trucks. Hot on the heels of this redesign came Chevrolet's first full-size 4x4, the Blazer, in 1969. The suspension arrangement on the Blazer was to use tapered single-leaf springs at the front and multi-leaf springs at the rear. The 4x4 Blazer base model was powered by an in-line six-cylinder engine although V8s were optional, as were manual or automatic transmissions, power steering, power brakes and a removable fibreglass hardtop. The colours, exterior trim, interior trim and general equipment were not dissimilar to the K10 4x4

pickup models. 4x2 Blazers were produced from 1970 onwards but proved less popular than the 4x4 models. There was little further change until 1972 when Isuzu of Japan supplied mini-pickups badged as Chevy LUVs, the LUV designation standing for Light Utility Vehicle. The LUV did well and more than 21,000 were sold in the period March–December 1972. Still in production were the El Camino and various capacities of full-size pickups.

The half- and three-quarter-ton trucks were still offered with a 4x4 option from 1973, the same year as the 15-millionth truck was made by the company. Interior trim levels were offered in a range of Custom, Custom Deluxe, Cheyenne and Cheyenne Super and sales topped the 920,000 mark. Despite the oil crisis of 1973 the 454-cubic inch (7440-cc) engine was introduced to immediate acclaim. The next year, the interior packages were renamed Silverado and Scottsdale which helped to confirm Chevrolet's dominance in the light 4x4 truck market.

The Blazer continued to prove popular as a full-size sport utility throughout the seventies. It was available in both C10 and K10 configurations, the differences, as usual, being two-wheel-drive and four-wheel-drive transmissions, although both variants had a 106.5-inch (271-cm) wheelbase. The 4x4 Blazer was marketed as the vehicle 'to take you where you want to go'. It had, in one interior configuration – according to the manufacturer – seating for five and 14.1 cubic feet (0.40 cubic metres) of space and a roll bar was fitted as standard.

In 1977 the company saw sales exceed one million per year and after 60 years of manufacture Chevrolet had made 21,850,083 trucks. The LUV put Chevrolet firmly into the mini-truck market and maintained its position there for almost a decade until the introduction of the Chevrolet S10 in 1981. The 1977 Chevy LUV was available in two wheelbases, 102.4 and 117.9 inches (260 and 300cm) and was, according to the sales brochure for that year, 'tough enough to be a Chevy'. The LUV was powered by a four-cylinder 80-bhp engine and according to the estimates of the Environmental Protection Agency (EPA) returned 34mpg (12km/l) on the highway and 24mpg (8km/l) in urban use. Numerous options were available, including the Mighty Mike decal package, a rear step bumper, automatic transmission, air-conditioning and AM/FM radio. Interior trim

LEFT
The fender emblem indicates that
the truck is an Apache and from
the 32 it is possible to tell that it is
one of the 3200 Series, a half-ton
longbed with a 123.25-inch
(313-cm) wheelbase. The badge was
one of the few differences to exist
between 1958 and 1959 models.

levels included the more luxurious Mikado package with a further
option of high-backed bucket seats in place of the bench seat.

The full size Chevy pickups were completely redesigned for
1973 and featured squared-off wheel arches, sculpted sides, a
roomier cab with a larger area of glass and an egg-crate radiator
grille. Trim levels available included Custom, Custom Deluxe,
Cheyenne and Cheyenne Super. For 1974 full-time 4x4 was
available in the four-wheel-drive models through use of the
NP203 transfer case in V8 models. California emissions
legislation meant that the in-line six-cylinder engine was not
available in that state. For 1975 the 400-cubic inch (6555-cc)
displacement small block V8 was added to the list of optional
engines and the NP203 transfer case became standard on all V8
automatic transmission models. The manual models retained the
conventional part-time system with locking hubs. In the interior
the Custom trim level was deleted making the Custom Deluxe the
base trim. K30 4x4 one-ton models were added to the Chevrolet
line-up in 1977 and with them the bonus cab and crew cab
models. The grille was redesigned and power windows were
added to the list of available options. 1978 saw the redesign of the
chassis to make space for the fitment of catalytic converters,
initially required in California. The grille was redesigned again in

OPPOSITE
Like many manufacturers, Chevrolet
offered its pickups in a variety of
forms including pickups, chassis-
cabs and stakebed trucks. This 1959
Chevrolet Apache is a restored
example of the latter and is now
fitted with custom wheels. Otherwise,
it is as it left the factory.

1979 and in 1980 the NP203 transfer case was discontinued meaning that all 4x4 Chevrolet pickups again featured a part-time 4x4 transmission arrangement using an NP205 transfer case. The Silverado models were given rectangular headlights but the major changes came for 1981.

In this year, the front-end sheetmetal was redesigned, as was the interior. Numerous power train changes were made including the fitment of the upgraded NP208 transfer case on 4x4 models and the introduction as an option of the 454-cubic inch (7440-cc) big block into the K models along with a four-speed manual overdrive transmission designed especially for it. The Cheyenne trim level was discontinued leaving Custom Deluxe, Scottsdale and Silverado trim specifications. The diesel transmission was available with other engines from 1984 onwards and in 1985 a V6 engine replaced the in-line six as the standard base engine and the grille was redesigned again – the seventh grille since 1973. Chevrolet made few changes to its trucks in 1986 as the new series was to be introduced in 1987 when 4x4 models would be designated V rather than K models.

The 1979 range of Chevrolet trucks were the C- and K-Series pickups, crew cab pickups, fleetside sport pickups and Big Dooleys (a larger capacity truck with dual rear wheels). A range of vans included the basic, the sportvan, the nomad van and a caravan. In addition to these there were the Suburban and Blazer models in two- and four-wheel-drive variants. This range was complemented by the Chevy LUV and the El Camino models. For the eighties the company adopted a new strategy and ceased manufacture of heavy duty trucks, preferring to concentrate on the medium- and light-duty markets. The S10 of 1982 was a compact that replaced the LUV and was available in two- and later four-wheel-drive.

The 1980 range of Chevrolet trucks was as large as ever and included two- and four-wheel-drive fleetside and stepside models as well as two- and four-wheel-drive Fleetside Sport and Stepside Sport models, two- and four-wheel-drive crew cab and bonus cab models, two- and four-wheel-drive chassis-cab models for specialist rear bodies such as wrecker trucks and the C10 diesel pickup and the heavy-duty BIG-10 pickup. 'Name the job there's truck here to match' said Chevrolet. Four trim packages were listed, Standard Custom Deluxe, Scottsdale, Cheyenne and

Phil Townend's 1959 Chevrolet Apache truck. It is a Model 3104, a 114-inch (290-cm) wheelbase half-ton stepside pickup.

OPPOSITE
A French registered American truck photographed in England. It is a 1963 Chevrolet truck that has been mildly customized. The whole vehicle has been lowered and fitted with custom wheels and resprayed deep red.

LEFT
A stock V8-powered 1967 Chevrolet truck, still in use in Greeley, Colorado 30 years after it was made.

Silverado. The latter was the most luxurious.

Over the course of the next decade the market shifted considerably and the sport truck became one of mainstream America's major purchases. The compact S10 was at the forefront of this trend. By 1991 the S10 and C-Series pickups and their respective Blazer and Suburban derivatives were as important as each other in the Chevrolet model line-up. The new for the nineties generation of C- and K-Series trucks were available with petrol and diesel engines, short- and long-load boxes, regular and extended cabs, and in three levels of trim, namely Cheyenne, Scottsdale and Silverado. There was a similar degree of choice for purchasers of the S10 compact pickup with the exception of the diesel-powered variant. The trim levels were known as Standard and Tahoe and there was an additional Baja off-road trim package for 4x4 models. The S10 Blazer came in two- or four-door models with choice of 4x2 and 4x4 transmissions and featured an Electronic Fuel Injection (EFI) V6 engine. Trim levels were as the S10. The full-size Blazer was V8 petrol- or diesel-powered with a choice of Scottsdale or Silverado trim and either two- or four-wheel-drive. The APV (All Purpose Vehicle) was a new addition to the Chevrolet light truck range and available were the Astro passenger van, the Lumina APV and the Sportvan. A spectacular Sport Truck from Chevrolet completed the 1991 range. Finished in Onyx Black was the 454 SS which was a 454 cubic inch (7440cc) V8-powered C1500 fleetside pickup.

ABOVE
The 4x4 Chevy pickup is a popular vehicle in the United States and often customized like this one photographed in Wheatland, Wyoming. It has been fitted with a rollbar, larger wheels and tyres, and a number of KC Daylighter spotlights. Bonanza (RIGHT) is a specification level.

OPPOSITE
Bill Smith's 1995 extended cab Chevrolet V8 pickup shows the way pickup design has evolved into the nineties.

Chapter 2
DODGE

Dodge's beginnings were in the second decade of the 20th century and it is famous for such machines as the mighty Power Wagon and the Ram.

RIGHT
A 1937 Dodge pickup street-rod. It has been fitted with a V8 engine and lowered at the front as well as being fitted with custom wheels and tyres of different sizes to give it the nose-down stance favoured by many street-rodders.

OPPOSITE
To meet demand for new pickups in the immediate post-war years, Dodge reintroduced its pre-war WC Series trucks with only minimal changes. Models such as this, seen in Steamboat Springs, Colorado, then ran for several years until a new range could be introduced for 1948.

The Dodge brothers began by making automobiles and became seriously involved in the manufacture of commercial-bodied variants during World War I. General John Pershing was so impressed with the Dodge car used during his campaigns in Mexico against Pancho Villa that he ordered his army staff to use them, as a result of which Dodge began to build a variety of commercial vehicles for use as troop-carriers, ambulances and light trucks. The first civilian Dodge commercial was basically a civilianized version of the screen-sided panel van built for the U.S. Army and went on sale in 1917. There then followed a period when another company was involved in the production of Dodge commercials. From 1921 Dodge had an agreement with a company called Graham to market its trucks (which used Dodge parts) through Dodge dealers. By 1923 there were Dodge passenger cars with Graham commercial bodies – an arrangement that remained unchanged until 1927, although several types of machine were marketed in this way. There were changes, however, when Walter P. Chrysler acquired Dodge in June 1928. He changed the name of the trucks back to Dodge, sanctioned the fitting of the four-cylinder Plymouth engine and production of these machines continued until 1933.

New for 1933 was a range of trucks completely designed by Chrysler. The range featured an in-line six-cylinder engine – a feature that would endure until the sixties – and the car-like styling of the time. The new models were again redesigned in 1936, now based on a ladder-type chassis, and yet again in 1939 when the company opened a new truck plant.

The outbreak of World War II saw the production of a range of military vehicles, including a three-quarter-ton 4x4 chassis that served as the basis for weapons-carriers, ambulances and command cars. This vehicle was such a success that a version of it was introduced post-war for the civilian market and was known as the Power Wagon and the model name was used on a variety of pickups from then on. The all-new post-war Dodges appeared in 1948 – the Series B models; the B-1-B was a half-ton, the B-1-C a three-quarter-ton and the B-1-D a one-ton (1,016kg). The company made a number of upgrades and options available throughout the fifties, including automatic transmission, column shifters, grilles, instrument panels as well as upgraded cab styling and even a variation on the cargo box.

Sales of Dodge trucks in this period were interesting; the years 1946 and 1947 were spectacular but there were drops in 1950 and 1953. But, despite the otherwise increasing sales, figures for 1947 would not be surpassed until 1968 because of the decline in sales of the late fifties. The company's market share fell to an all-time low in 1961 before seeing an upward trend.

The next major restyle came in 1957 when the front end was restyled and the Sweptside D100 was introduced, larger capacity V8s (315 cubic inches/ 5162cc) were fitted and even the utilitarian Power Wagon was redesigned although the original one was still available. The redesigned cabs featured a one-piece rear-hinged hood and were changed slightly for the next year when double headlights were fitted.

The sixties were important for Dodge when it built a complete and comprehensive line of pickups and was among the first to switch to alternators. The redesigned cabs were lower and wider than the ones before and were mounted on new chassis with different wheelbases. Though the next year's revisions were minimal, switches from single to dual headlights and back again were typical. In the range were sweptline pickups, sweptline Power Wagons and crew cab Power Wagons. There were a

RIGHT
The Dodge WC/WD Series trucks were sold in a variety of forms including chassis-cab, stakebed, panel van, platform truck and regular pickup. They were also sold in two wheelbases and three payloads. This is the half-ton pickup based on the 116-inch (295-cm) wheelbase chassis.

OPPOSITE LEFT
The Dodge Power Wagon was a strictly utilitarian 4x4 truck. This example was photographed in Wheatland, Wyoming, where it was used for many years on fencing projects.

OPPOSITE RIGHT
Alison Thomas owns this early fifties Dodge, restored as though it belonged to a fifties speed shop.

number of derivatives such as the fully enclosed Power Wagon, known as a Town Wagon, of 1962.

With minimal styling changes the sixties trucks ran for the whole decade and the redesign came at the beginning of the seventies. Independent front suspension, yet lower and wider cabs and a new interior were part of this redesign. The list of available options increased in length to include components such as electronic ignition and new to the industry was the club cab (an extended cab) model. The grille was redesigned for 1974 and the Ramcharger, a 4x4 sport utility, was launched. Innovation continued throughout the seventies when full-time 4x4 systems, a 4x2 Ramcharger and a dual rear-wheel arrangement option for one-ton pickups of 1975 and 1976 were followed by the Li'l Red Truck as a type of factory custom truck of 1978. Running parallel to this were the more usual year-by-year alterations such as variations in headlights, grilles and trim. An optional Mitsubishi diesel engine was available and Dodge later imported two models of Mitsubishi pickup.

The start of the eighties was low-key, with minimal changes, but the arrival of a new chairman – Lee Iacocca – at Chrysler made headline news. Changes to grilles, lights and interiors continued with the introduction of egg-crate grilles. Dodge was gradually shifting, however, to more aerodynamic pickups and a down-sized model, the front-wheel-drive Rampage, a sport truck.

LEFT
A 1995 V10 Dodge Ram pickup. This
truck has an 8-litre engine and
produces 300 bhp @ 4,000 rpm.

OPPOSITE LEFT ABOVE
Dean Miller's Pro-Street 1971 Dodge
is powered by a Mopar 440 V8 and
features a narrowed Chrysler rear
axle, a Mustang independent front
suspension assembly, and Weld
Racing wheels. The body has been
tubbed to suit the tyres and the roof
of the truck has been chopped
3 inches (8cm).

OPPOSITE LEFT BELOW
A 1996 Dodge Ram photographed in
Steamboat Springs, Colorado.

Chapter 3
FORD

Model Ts, Model As and Model Bs, Ford has long produced pickup trucks,
including the legendary F-1s and F-100s of the late forties and fifties.

ord's most famous early commercial vehicle is undoubtedly the Model T but the story actually starts slightly earlier. In 1905 Ford offered what it described as the Delivery Car, basically a Model C automobile with a delivery-type body. It was discontinued in 1906 and between then and 1911 the only Ford trucks made were car conversions. The Model T Delivery Car was introduced in 1912 and was followed by the Model TT – a Model T Ton, i.e. a truck of one-ton (1,016kg) capacity. There was also a range of Model T Roadster pickups and some specifically constructed panel vans. The line was expanded drastically in 1928 with the arrival of the Model A and subsequently the Model AA, half-ton series which were available as both roadster and closed cab pickups. By 1931 there were 31 different colours available, including Yukon Yellow, Menelous Orange and Rubellite Red.

New for 1932 was the Model B, subsequently nicknamed 'the Deuce' which despite being launched in the Depression became one of the most famous American cars of the thirties. One of the reasons for this is that it came with an L-head V8 engine (a flathead four was an option) which endowed it with considerable performance that would subsequently endear it to the hot-rodders. Chevrolet introduced a six-cylinder engine in 1929 and sales soared to the extent that they were outselling Ford. Henry Ford consequently decided to raise the stakes and introduce a V8 model. V8s themselves were not new and were already in use in luxury cars such as Lincolns but they were not available in mass-produced cars and trucks. The problem of offering a mass-produced, and therefore cheap, V8 lay in the difficulty of casting a single unit of crankcase block and cylinder banks as one unit. Up until then the V8 was cast in three parts, machined, and fitted together. Against the background of the Depression, times were desperate and Ford closed a number of his autoplants and laid off approximately 75,000 workers. The design of the new Ford range progressed under Edsel Ford and Joe Galamb and engineer Gene Farkas redesigned the chassis, eventually solving the casting problem and making the cheap V8 a reality. The 1932 Ford range appeared though sales were slow in ten car variants and four commercials. The latter four included a sedan delivery, a Murray and Baker-Raulang-bodied station wagon and two pickups. The

OPPOSITE
A factory stock Ford Model A closed cab pickup truck. Ford designated it the Model 82B and made in excess of 86,000 in 1930. Such a truck retailed in that year at $435.

LEFT
An early thirties Ford closed cab pickup. The styling, introduced in 1932, ran on for 1933 and 1934 whereas that of the cars was changed for 1933 with, among other things, a different grille shell. The big news from Ford in 1932 was the introduction of the flathead V8 which was announced for Ford's whole range although it was not available for the commercial variants until part-way through the 1932 model year.

Detail of the 1932/33 Ford truck. The grille shell and headlamps (RIGHT) have become classics and these models are enormously popular as street-rods. The stock interior (FAR RIGHT) featured dash-mounted instruments and a large diameter steering wheel. The spare wheel (OPPOSITE LEFT) was carried in a well especially formed in the fender. The hub cap bears the Ford V8 logo.

OPPOSITE RIGHT
Ford regularly redesigned the front-end sheetmetal of its commercial models for new model years. The grille used on 1938 and 1939 Ford pickup trucks was of a rounded distinctive shape.

pickups were a Murray-bodied open cab and a closed cab truck. The sedan delivery (with a single side-hung door rather than a pair as in a panel van), the Station Wagon Woody, and open cab pickup were built in small numbers – a total of 2,371 for all three. But 14,259 of the closed cab pickups rolled off the line although they were almost all four-cylinder-powered because the V8 was not available for them until late in the model year. For 1933/34 the sedan deliveries followed the lines of the redesigned cars but the roadster and closed cab pickups remained more like the 1932 models in appearance.

A redesign came for 1935, the year that Fords were the best-selling cars and trucks in the United States. The restyle incorporated a new, narrower grille, a longer hood, and more rounded fenders. This design was only slightly revised for 1936 with minor changes to the wheels and radiator grille shell. An unusual truck appeared in 1937, a standard coupé with a pickup body introduced to compete with Chevrolet who had introduced something similar the previous year. It was a poor seller for both companies and Ford discontinued it at the end of that model year while Chevrolet persevered with its version until the outbreak of World War II.

For 1938 Ford offered a range of one-ton trucks to complement its existing half-ton line and made the range even more comprehensive for 1939 when a three-quarter-ton range was added. These models featured a rounded radiator grille, even more rounded fenders, and steel wheels instead off the laced wire types used until this time. New for 1940 was the Forty Ford range which, with hindsight, can be seen as some of Ford's most handsome trucks ever. The trucks featured styling which was akin to the cars of that year, with graceful hoods that finished almost to a point. The rear sheetmetal varied depending on the type of vehicle, panel van, pickup or stakebed truck. There were half-, three-quarter- and one-ton variants which had 112- and 122-inch (285- and 310-cm) wheelbases. The coupé pickup reappeared for 1941 and the radiator grille and hood designs varied according to different payloads. Marmon-Herrington offered a 4x4 conversion to the three-quarter-ton Model 11D pickup. The sheetmetal was redesigned again for 1942 and the company then turned its efforts to winning World War II. One of Ford's contributions to the Allied cause was to turn some of its production capability over to Willys MB Jeeps because Willys did not have the production capacity required. The Ford-assembled

Jeeps were designated Ford GPW and the company also produced an amphibian variant of the same vehicle which was designated GPA. The Model GC was a military specification 4x4 pickup truck.

For the immediate post-war trucks, Ford kept the design features of the last pre-war models including the so-called Waterfall grille. It was so described because of its row of vertical bars. The post-war trucks did feature a number of improvements over those before the war but 1948 saw the introduction of Ford's first completely new post-war truck. The styling had been radically altered. The headlights were now set into the recessed horizontally barred grille and the fenders were squared off and joined across the top of the radiator grille below the hood. The cab was larger in all three dimensions and rubber-mounted to the chassis. The new half-ton truck was known as the F-1 and was available as the F-2 and F-3 as a three-quarter-tonner. The basic style endured through 1952 although the grille was radically redesigned for 1951.

The F-100, as the new model was tagged, was introduced on 13 March 1953 with a sleeker and more modern appearance than anything that had gone before. It was available in many variants

of which the F-100 was the one-ton model and was available as platform/stake truck, stepside and as the F10D3 straight six-powered unit or the F10R3 which was the V8-powered version. Larger-capacity versions were the three-quarter-ton F-250 and F-350 and larger again was the F-500. Once again the basic design was to last several years with only minor upgrades in terms of grille changes, body panel variations, interior changes and similar. The overall styling change was made in 1957 and in the same year the Ford Ranchero made its debut. This combined car and truck features to offer a car-type cab and front sheetmetal

with a pickup load bed between the rear fenders. Similar models continued through 1958 and 1959 although in the latter year the base model Ranchero was discontinued, leaving only the top-of-the range Custom Ranchero available. The F-100 by now had single headlights, a horizontally-barred grille and a wrap-around windshield. The rear bed was described as styleside and had the wheels within the bodywork rather than being of stepside design. This lasted several years into the sixties through a number of minor upgrades, such as the face-lift for 1962 and new grilles for 1964 and 1965.

New for 1966 was the change of base for the Ranchero. Instead of the Falcon platform it was now based on the Fairlane. Ford also unveiled the four-wheel-drive Bronco for 1966 in three guises, roadster pickup, sport utility pickup and wagon. The Bronco in various configurations would remain an important part of Ford's range for years to come in much the same way as the F-100 pickup. The F-100 was restyled for 1967 but remained available as styleside, flareside, chassis-cab and platform/stake and there were two longer wheelbase models. The F-250 remained as the three-quarter-ton variant available with as many body types and two crew-cabs, namely a styleside and a chassis-cab. The one-ton F-350 was offered as a flareside pickup and chassis/cab but also in two wheelbases with platform and stakebed bodies. There were also long wheelbase F-350 crew cabs in styleside and chassis-cab variants.

The Bronco and Ranchero models continued through 1968, 1969 and into the 1970s in similar configurations although the body styles of the Ranchero would subsequently be redesigned several times in keeping with the passenger car-type styling. Four-wheel-drive transmissions were available as an extra cost option. In 1968, for example, the 4x4 system added an extra $645 to the cost of both the F-100 and F-250 models. In that year production of the entire range which had been introduced in the autumn of 1967 was a fraction less than 415,000 vehicles.

In 1972 the style of construction used in the Ranchero models was changed; it now featured a separate chassis and body to make it bigger and stronger in contrast to the previous unit construction. A sport version was known as the Ranchero GT Sedan-Pickup and the Squire variant featured imitation wood panels along the sides and a number of other trim detail upgrades.

ABOVE
Ford pickups were redesigned for 1940 when the hood became noticeably pointed and the headlamps were recessed into the fenders.
RIGHT
This V8 truck has been fitted with custom wheels, has had the front bumper removed, and the hood louvred.
OPPOSITE
In the post-war years the styling changed again. This 1950 Ford F-1 has noticeably more angular fenders back and front. It too is running on custom wheels.

OPPOSITE AND LEFT
Ford's first really new post-war pickup was the F-1 of 1948 with the distinctive horizontally-barred grille. The hood release catch is operated by the horizontal bar in the right-side hood vent. Altered in only very minor ways, this grille lasted through the 1950 truck range. Much of the truck itself endured two years longer and with a completely redesigned grille the basic shape remained until late 1952.

The base models were powered by an in-line six while the base GT models featured a V8. There were numerous V8 options, too, that included 302-, 351-, 400-, and 429-cubic inch (4949-, 5752-, 6555-, and 7030-cc) displacement engines as well as both manual and automatic transmissions. The styling changes to the F-100 and F-250 models were more limited in their scope and were restricted to such things as redesigned grilles and interior detail upgrades.

The positions were reversed for 1973 when the F-100 and F-250 were given considerably more changes than the Ranchero models. The hood was redesigned with a flatter face and the cab was made longer to provide storage behind the seats; the sides of the body detail changed from convex to concave. There were chassis-cab, flareside and styleside variants, production of the first two models totalling less than 6,000 while those of styleside exceeded 457,000. The story for the F-250 models was similar in terms of styling and proportion of production run although the total of all three variants was approximately 198,000 vehicles. Of

the one-ton F-350 models though, the largest production were the 42,000 chassis-cab models, leaving a total of only 26,600 for all the other variants including styleside, chassis/cowl, platform, parcel van and P-400 models. This reflects the F-350's suitability for installation of specialist rear bodies for agricultural and industrial uses.

For 1974 Bronco and Ranchero production continued with only minor changes while the F-100, F-250 and F-350 styling remained unchanged although an extended cab model was made available and was known as the Super Cab. The Super Cab was available in all three payloads and almost 30,000 were produced in the first year. Ford production of the 1974 range which had been introduced on 1 September 1973 exceeded the one million mark for the calendar year and surpassed that of Chevrolet, allowing Ford to retain its position as number one.

The Ranchero went into 1975 unchanged although the Bronco was revised with a stronger rear axle reflecting its off-road use and later in the year was fitted with disc brakes on the

OPPOSITE
A 1951 Ford half-ton F-1 pickup. While the grille is different the remainder of the truck is very similar to the earlier model (*see page 45*). Like many American pickup trucks, this Florida F-1 has been fitted with custom wheels and resprayed in a custom colour.

LEFT
The Ford range of light trucks was redesigned for 1953 and the transition to a wider, flatter-looking fender and hood-line made. This basic shape would also endure for several years with only minor changes to grilles and trim.

RIGHT
The 1959 Ford trucks, such as this hard-worked California example, featured much flatter panels and more angular lines. Detail changes included a move to twin headlamps. The basic design lasted into 1960, although the FORD name was substituted on the leading edge of the hood for a smaller emblem and the grille was redesigned.

OPPOSITE
A similar pattern was seen in the mid-sixties pickups. The 1965 models (TOP LEFT) became the 1966 models (FAR RIGHT) with a redesign to the grille and other minor changes rather than a complete redesign. The two trucks are, however, stepside and styleside models respectively. The hood emblems (BELOW LEFT) show that the truck was V8-powered and it was varied from model year to year.

front axle. Exterior styling remained unchanged on the range of pickups and only minor upgrades were made elsewhere. The F-150 – a slightly heavier-duty version of the F-100 – was introduced to the Ford range. The range continued as it was with a minor face-lift for the year of America's bicentennial, 1976.

The 1977 Ranchero was redesigned to incorporate stacked rectangular headlights while the other Ford trucks continued almost as before. The variety of options, variations, and body types meant that it made possible vehicles such as an F-150

Ranger XLT Flareside 4x4 Pickup. XLT was a trim level and flareside was what Ford called their stepside models.

For 1978 the Bronco was completely restyled and now closely resembled the full-size Ford pickups which had also been restyled for this model year. The grille was set higher and featured a rectangular design, the amber lights being set below the headlamps, and a new bumper installed. The types of cab and transmission in 4x2 or 4x4 configurations were retained, as were the F-100, F-150, F-250 and F-350 model designations. This

continued for 1979 although the trucks were equipped with rectangular headlights.

At the start of the new decade, Ford advertised its F-100 as 'the first new truck of the eighties' and unveiled redesigned models, including a number with custom paint options with contrasting panels. The model designations remained unchanged so it was possible to buy a Ford Heavy Half-Ton F-150 Custom Flareside 4x4 Pickup. The 4x4 models featured a new front suspension system, the Twin-Traction Beam Independent

suspension. The Ranchero pickup was dropped from the Ford range that year. Sales of the early eighties models dropped because of the poor state of the economy and Ford continued with its compact Mazda-built Courier pickups and turned some of its attention to more fuel-efficient vehicles. Styling of the F-range trucks remained the same although minor upgrades included removing the word Ford from the front edge of the hood and installing the famous blue logo in the centre of the grille. In March 1982, the down-sized Ranger pickup made its debut with styling

OPPOSITE
A much modified Ford F-Series pickup on Daytona Beach, Florida. the large wheels and aggressive tyres assist off-road potential in boggy terrain.

LEFT
A 1996 Ford F-250 crew-cab in Colorado. The crew-cab concept became popular during the nineties because of the additional storage the extension to the cab offered.

RIGHT
Martha Richmond's Ford F-150 XLT
Ranger Super Cab pickup. XLT is the
specification level while Ranger was
the name given to a number of
Ford's compact vehicles.

OPPOSITE
A 1997 Ford F-150 XLT Super Cab
pickup. F-150 is Ford's long-running
designation and refers to a payload
that goes back to the F-100
designation used in the immediate
post-war years. F-100 became F-150
when the basic payload was
increased.

similar to the F-100. New for 1984 was the down-sized Bronco II
sport utility based along similar lines to the Ranger pickup. The
F-100 was discontinued with the F-150 becoming the base model
in a range that still included F-250 and F-350 pickups.

By the middle of the decade the Ranger and Bronco II were
established in Ford's range of light-duty trucks, along with the
full-size F-150, F-250 and F-350 models. The big news for 1986

was not of the pickup range but of the Ford vans when the
Aerostar XL passenger van was introduced. Bronco IIs and
Ranger pickups remained in the range as did the F-150, F-250
and F-350 models and, after the disappointing sales of the early
years of the decade, Ford had both a record sales year and
regained the number one position in the U.S. auto sales charts.

Chapter 4
GMC

General Motors has a history of building pickup trucks that stretches right back to 1911. The styling reflected the trends of the day and created machines such as the classic 1962 GMC three-quarter-ton Wideside.

This massive corporation began in a small way. In 1903 William C. Durant took control of Buick and in 1908 founded his General Motors empire which absorbed a number of early car and truck makers. In 1911 the truck names were changed to GMC and Chevrolet was acquired during World War I; another merger followed in 1925 and yet another in 1943.

The General Motors Corporation began light truck production in the second decade of the 20th century, producing a range of trucks prior to World War I. Its early models earned a reputation for both ruggedness and reliability and during the war the Model 16 One Tonner became the basis for many U.S. Army ambulances and in the years after the war became the basis for the GMC K-Series. Production of GMC trucks continued through the twenties with engines by companies such as Buick who supplied GMC with an in-line six-cylinder motor. Towards the end of the decade GMC offered a line of trucks, the T-11, based on a Pontiac design that had only been offered for a single year and in this model the Pontiac engine was installed. A new model of truck, the T-19, was introduced in 1928 and demonstrated that

GMC was making progress in its design of trucks. The T-19 was manufactured in large numbers, some 20,000 examples being made in 1928 and 1929. In 1933 GMC began to produce Buick engines specifically for its trucks with bore and stroke altered to make them more suitable for use in commercial vehicles. These engines, in different displacements, had production runs of more than 20 years. It was during the thirties that the company really got into the swing of light truck manufacture and began to produce trucks with modern styling. The early thirties models had styling comparable with the Fords of the day; cabs had vertical windshields and hoods were long with louvred sides. The range for 1932 included the T-11 half-ton, T-15 three-quarter-ton, T-15AA and T-17A one-ton models. The range was redesigned for 1936 and again for 1937.

The T-14 of 1937 was a half-ton truck powered by a 230-cubic inch (3769-cc) displacement in-line six-cylinder engine. The front end featured a vertical grille with bullet-shaped headlights positioned between the fenders and the sides of the hood and the remainder of the truck was in a basic configuration that would endure for several years. The T-16L was a three-quarter-ton version of the same model and the FL-16 was a walk-in delivery van version. A similar range was offered for 1938 although the headlights were now mounted on the sides of the hood.

The range was redesigned for 1939; windshields became two-piece and although the grille remained vertical it was redesigned to incorporate heavier horizontal inserts. The company offered four six-cylinder-powered half-ton models on a 113.5-inch (288-cm) wheelbase and three similarly-engined models with a 123.75-inch (314-cm) wheelbase. The half-tonners were designated Series AC-100 and AC-102 trucks while the greater payload

models were the AC-150, AC-250 and ACL-300 the three-quarter and one-ton (1,016-kg) models. AC-250 models had the 123.75-inch wheelbase and the AC-300 and ACL-300 models were based on a 133-inch (338-cm) wheelbase. In the various capacities there were chassis, chassis-cab, pickup and panel van models and in the larger capacity trucks there were also platform, stakebed and express models. In 1937 almost 35,000 GMC trucks were registered. This entire range was developed for the 1940 model year and walk-in delivery vans of a forward control design (where the driver sits over or forward of the front axle) were added to the range. The design received a few minor changes

This late thirties GMC is owned by Timmerman's, a German motorcycle shop specializing in Indian bikes. The fender lights of the truck have been substituted for those of an Indian Chief motorcycle.

including a redesigned dash and sealed beam headlights.

In the few years prior to American involvement in World War II the GMC trucks were redesigned again and most of them redesignated as CC-Series trucks. The redesign moved the headlights out onto the fenders, saw a new horizontal barred grille fitted and incorporated the sidelights into the tops of the headlight cowls. The styling remained the same for 1942 models until production was suspended for the duration of the war. Among others, GMC produced a vast number of the famous 6x6 'deuce and a half' 2½-ton trucks for the allied armies. These trucks were available in soft- and hard-cab models with a cab not dissimilar in design to that of the CC-Series half-ton trucks.

In 1946 GMC resumed civilian production with light trucks that were almost identical to the pre-war models in order to give its staff time to design a new series of light trucks. The new models were the FC-Series which featured GMC's all-new Advance-Design styling which was smooth and rounded. The grille comprised a series of horizontal bars and the GMC logo was affixed to the hood above the grille. The headlights were mounted in the fenders, adding to the streamlined appearance while underneath, the front suspension was redesigned. Because the new design of truck had been introduced part-way through 1947 it continued to be marketed throughout 1948. With only minor improvements the design continued into 1949, the gas tank now positioned inside the cab on all models so that the tank filler cap was located at the right rear of the cab. The half-ton FC-101 models were standard on a 116-inch (295-cm) wheelbase and the range included a chassis, a chassis-cab, a pickup, a panel van, a canopy express and a suburban. The FC-102 models were also rated as half-tons but were based on a 125.25-inch (318-cm) wheelbase. Also on this wheelbase were the three-quarter-ton FC-152 models. Both FC-102 and FC-152 models were available as chassis, chassis-cab, pickup and stakebed models. There were few changes for 1950 although a few of the options were altered and the horsepower of the 228-cubic inch (3736-cc) in-line six-cylinder engine was boosted slightly. It was the same story for 1951, 1952 and 1953 as only minor changes were made leading up to the redesigns for 1954 and 1955.

In 1954 the GMC light trucks received the most extensive redesign since 1948 although the continuing style was still

apparent. The grille design remained familiar though slightly altered, the front fenders were redesigned, the cabs now had one-piece windshields and the cargo box and tailgate were remodelled. This design continued into 1955 because, although GMC trucks and cars were due for a complete redesign for 1955, GMC was unable to redesign all its vehicles during the autumn of 1954 for the beginning of the 1955 sales year. As a result, the new and completely redesigned GMC (and Chevrolet) trucks did not go on sale until the spring of 1955.

The new trucks were considerably more angular than their predecessors. The front end featured a two-bar grille reminiscent of cars of the era and was complemented by hooded headlamps and a massive chromed fender. The GMC logo, in stylized form, was mounted on the lower portion of the hood front. The cab was redesigned to incorporate a wrap-around windshield and the higher front fender line ran right through the cab and doors. The comprehensive range of new designs were designated as follows:

ABOVE
The truck was redesigned twice in 1955, this being the first redesign with the larger hood emblem Following this, the trucks became more angular in appearance.

OPPOSITE
A GMC Series 150 three-quarter-ton truck from the early fifties with a 125.25-inch (318-cm) wheelbase. Half-ton models were also available with the same wheelbase and also a shorter 116-inch (295-cm) version.

Series 100, half-ton 114-inch (290-cm) wheelbase six-cylinder models; Series 102, half-ton 123.25-inch (313-cm) wheelbase six-cylinder models; Series 100-8, half-ton 114-inch wheelbase V8 models; Series 102-8, 123.25-inch wheelbase V8 models; Series 150, three-quarter-ton 123.25-inch wheelbase six-cylinder models; Series 150-8, three-quarter-ton 123.25-inch wheelbase V8 models; Series PM-151, three-quarter-ton 104-inch (264-cm) wheelbase six-cylinder models; Series PM-153, one-ton 137-inch (348-cm) wheelbase models; Series 251, one-ton 114-inch wheelbase six-cylinder models; Series 252 one-ton 123.25-inch wheelbase six-cylinder models; Series 253, one-ton 135-inch (343-cm) wheelbase six-cylinder models. There were also V8 variants of the Series 251, 252 and 253 trucks. Of these various models registrations for the 1955 calendar year totalled 84,877 vehicles.

There was little change for the 1956 models although the V8 models were no longer listed as a separate series – the V8 simply became an option. The engines were increased in displacement to 269.5 and 316.6 cubic inches (4416 and 5188cc) for the six- and eight-cylinder units respectively. The redesigned grille was the only visibly obvious change for 1957. For 1958 the range was redesigned in several small ways; a wideside steel pickup body was introduced and less decorative hub caps, dual headlights and a new grille changed the exterior appearance. The front fender was exchanged for a less ostentatious version for 1959 and the results of another redesign appeared in 1960.

The new trucks featured a more modern cab that had a lower overall height. A concave styling feature ran along the sides of the fenders, cab and bed. The full-width hood had lights in pods on either side while the headlights were dual and mounted in the grille. The rear of the cab featured an overhang while the front included a wrap-around windshield. Underneath the trucks were also to be found a number of new features including a new front suspension system, a redesigned frame that was both stronger and lighter, and an optional V6 engine of 305-cubic inch (4998-cc) displacement. Four-wheel-drive was an option at $650 extra and three payloads were available. The P1000-Series were the half-ton models while the P1500 and P2500 were the three-quarter and one-ton models respectively. The choice of body types across these ranges included chassis-cab, pickup, stakebed, panel, wideside and fenderside models. As GMC did not produce trucks

GMC offered its basic truck with various payloads. In the case of the larger capacity trucks, the axles and wheel sizes were different. This GMC features 20-inch (51-cm) wheels in place of the 16-inch (41-cm) used on the half- and three-quarter-ton models. The sheetmetal of the cab is the same as the smaller capacity models but the chassis is different. This truck was sold as a chassis-cab unit and was fitted with a specialist rear body by the Winter-Weiss Company of Denver, Colorado.

LEFT
A late seventies custom half-ton GMC stepside pickup. The American truck with German licence plates has been considerably lowered and fitted with a chrome roll bar. Other non-standard items include the alloy wheels. The logo GMC is pressed into the tailgate and the Custom Deluxe badge is indicative of a trim option.

on a strict model year basis the range did not necessarily change in the autumn of each year and the 1960 trucks went forward into 1961 completely unchanged though some styling changes were made for 1962. The hood was lowered and rounded off, eliminating the vents in the leading edge and a single long vent was positioned between the parking lights. Other minor changes included a change of hub caps and redesigned badges. This redesign also carried GMC through the 1963 model year. The year 1964 was notable for GMC's entry into the light van market although the cab of their range of pickups was redesigned to eliminate the wrap-around windshield in favour of one consisting of a piece of curved glass. With a few minor detail changes this truck remained in production until the end of 1966.

The GMC trucks for 1967 were completely redesigned in both styling and technical features to progress GMC's pickups. A number of safety features including seat belts, four-way flashing hazard lights and dual braking system were included as standard. The truck bodies were both more angular and more curved at the same time. The overall shape was more slab-sided but sharp radii had been eliminated in favour of rounded edges, giving a modern look to the trucks, and this was complemented by the simple bar grille and dual headlamps set in trims. Following this major redesign the changes for 1968 were minimal although larger displacement V8s were available. Changes were again minor for 1969 although the list of factory options was increased.

GMC launched a new product in 1970 in order to reap some

OPPOSITE
GMC termed trucks not possessing stepside beds, such as this one, 'wideside' models. New for 1960 was the P1000/1500 and 2500 series with the pinched-waist appearance created by the concave line that ran along the sides of the trucks. The side trim was an option and the truck was available in three payloads and four wheelbases. This is the 115-inch (292-cm) wheelbase half-ton model, the P1001.

ABOVE Greg Wolf's 1979 GMC fenderside (as GMC describes its stepside models) is more modified than it appears. It has been lowered 4 inches (10cm) at the front and 6 inches (15cm) at the rear. A Bell Tech front end has been installed to facilitate the front-end drop while at the rear it is achieved through use of different springs. The wheels and tyres are not the originals and a custom sliding rear-cab window has been fitted. The logo GMC is pressed into the tailgate and carried on the grille (ABOVE RIGHT) and sides. The Sierra Classic and 15 emblems (RIGHT) indicate that the truck is from GMC's 1500 Series and trimmed to the Sierra Classic specification.

benefit from the growing recreational market. The new truck was the GMC Jimmy. It took much of its styling from the GMC pickup truck range and was available in both two- and four-wheel-drive configurations with a removable hardtop over the rear load bed and front seats. It was designated C1550 and K1550, the prefix varying according to its transmission. C equates with the 4x2 and K the 4x4.

For the first years of the seventies the GMC trucks continued to receive only minor upgrades for each year but they, along with the Jimmy, were restyled for 1973 and again grilles and minor details changed for the following years as conventional trucks continued to share front sheetmetal with the Jimmy. The number of options increased, the High Sierra trim option, for example, adding wood grain-type panels to the sides of the GMC products. Crew cabs, suburbans, carryalls and similar variations on a theme continued to be added to the range and the K-prefix continued to indicate a 4x4 model. By 1977 it was possible to buy a GMC K3500 Crew Cab Wideside 4x4 Pickup, the 4x4 option adding $1248 to the price. Other options were also available, including the Desert Fox trim option of 1978 which reflected the popularity of off-road desert racing in the United States. Indy hauler trucks were also built to mark the GMC company's involvement with the Indy 500 when GMC supplied official speedway trucks during the famous race. There were a number of minor styling upgrades for 1979 that included alterations to the grille. For 1980 changes to the trucks were mainly cosmetic although the grille, square-patterned like an ice cube tray, remained. An option was the dual stacked rectangular headlamps either side of the grille in place of the single round one fitted as standard. The half-ton models retained an in-line six-cylinder engine as standard while the other base models had a V8. The programme of minor upgrades continued into the 1981 models; detail upgrades were made to the transmission of the 4x4 variants, for example, and the front sheetmetal of the Jimmys and pickups was redesigned to be more aerodynamic and therefore more fuel-efficient.

New for 1982 were the GMC S15 trucks on which work had begun in 1978 as a response to the increasing popularity of the smaller imported trucks such as the Isuzu badged as the Chevy

LUV. The S15 was similar in size to the LUV and by 1983 there were 4x4 and extended cab models available. The downsized Jimmy was based around the S15 and featured a tailgate and two doors on a 100.5-inch (255-cm) wheelbase and was four-wheel-drive. For 1984 the GMC Indy Hauler pickup was based on an S15 model. The full-size trucks continued into the mid-eighties with the same general appearance as previously although the programme of sequential upgrades continued. Suspension and engine were two areas where refinements were made. They continued in both wideside and fenderside variants and, reflecting increasing trends towards improved fuel efficiency, diesel options were included in the range.

A customized Extracab GMC. It has been lowered and painted with graphics and both these features emphasize the already long, modern lines of the truck.

Chapter 5
INTERNATIONAL HARVESTER

International Harvester differs slightly from its rivals in that it was essentially a manufacturer of agricultural machines who built a range of working trucks, including the S-120 models of 1956, and pioneered the sport utility vehicle with the Scout.

The International Harvester Corporation (IHC) had its beginnings in the McCormick reaper of 1831 which led to the formation of IHC in 1902. By 1907 production of commercial machines had begun and vehicles such as the Auto-Wagon appeared, featuring panel van and grain box bodies. Through the remainder of the decade the company produced a range of light trucks including utility wagons and panel vans but gradually shifted the entire emphasis to light trucks. A new line of conventional trucks was introduced in 1915 with payloads from three-quarter-ton upwards. Unusually, the radiator was placed behind the engine. The next new line of trucks was introduced in 1921 and was known as the S-Series. The S indicated speed trucks which were capable of 30mph (48km/h). Because of the machines' small size and their red finish they soon became known as the Red Babies. The IHC trucks were sold through 170 IHC farm equipment dealers – the trucks were nicknamed cornbinders – and in 1929 around 50,000 were sold.

During the thirties IHC used alphabetical designations for its trucks; the A series appeared between 1930 and 1932, the C from 1933 to 1934, and so on. There was no Model B – presumably because Ford was already using that designation at that time. The AW-1, for example, was a conventional three-quarter-ton truck, powered by a four-cylinder engine, and was available as either chassis, panel, pickup, canopy, screen or sedan delivery truck. The Model C series of 1935 included the C-1, C-10, C-20 and M-3. The C-1 models were the half-tonners in both 113- and 125-inch (287- and 318-cm) wheelbases. The C-10 models were three-quarter-ton trucks on a 133-inch (338-cm) wheelbase. The C-20s were larger trucks based on a 157-inch (399-cm) wheelbase and a maximum capacity of around $1\frac{1}{2}$ tons. The M-3 was a 133-inch wheelbase one-ton (1,016kg) truck.

IHC expanded in 1936 to include seven basic truck models within its range with styling similar to the 1935 models. This included a tall V-shaped grille, long hood with louvred sides, a tall cab and curved fenders that joined running-boards. The smaller displacement trucks used Waukesha four-cylinder engines while the larger models used an in-line six. A redesigned line of trucks – the D-Series – made their debut in the spring of 1937, their appearance being considerably altered with redesigned grilles, two-piece windshields and a fat-fendered appearance. The all-steel cab styling was referred to as turret-top. This new range helped IHC increase its lead over Dodge and retain its third position in sales in the United States with 30.22 per cent of the total truck market. This figure would drop to 10.24 per cent for 1938 but still leave IHC in third place. The trucks continued almost unchanged for 1939 and IHC figures improved slightly when it achieved 11.38 per cent of the total U.S. market.

IHC introduced its Model K truck in the latter part of 1940 for the 1941 model year. Styling was modern with integral fenders that incorporated headlights and a smaller vertical grille and rounded hood. The new series was powered by the Green Diamond in-line six-cylinder engine. With only minor changes this design took IHC up to the outbreak of war.

During World War II, IHC manufactured a range of machinery for military use including half-track vehicles for the allied armies. The company produced more than 13,000 International M-5 half-tracks at its Springfield plant. The company also made 'essential use' pickups for civilians who required transport in order to assist the war effort. Civilian production fully resumed in 1946 with the reintroduction of the K-Series. These trucks were redesignated the KB-Series with their redesign for 1947. Little had changed since the pre-war models

PAGE 64
A street-rodded International
Harvester pickup from 1938, in
Texas.

PAGE 65
A derelict KB-1 International
Harvester truck from 1949
photographed in Colorado.

RIGHT
A partially restored International
Harvester panel van from the early
forties. Most American
manufacturers offered panel van
variants of their light truck models.

OPPOSITE
This pickup is a similar model but
with the regular pickup bed. It differs
in details, such as the hood emblems,
as the two vehicles are from different
model years.

and not much else would until 1950.

In January 1950 the all-new L-Series trucks were unveiled. The trucks were completely restyled and re-engineered. The styling of the body now incorporated wide, flat fenders, a less rounded hood, and significant changes were made to both grille and trim. Beneath the hood was fitted a new in-line six-cylinder overhead valve engine. This style ran until 1953 when it was superseded by the R-Series, a somewhat modernized form of L-Series. The front end had been redesigned and was now concave with an oval aperture. A two-tone paint job was an option as was a model with a greater payload. The standard half-ton pickups were known as R-100 with an 115-inch (292-cm) wheelbase but the R-102 was the heavier truck based on the same wheelbase. The R-110 was the longer wheelbase variant, also available as the R-111 and R-112. These trucks remained in production until 1955 when the S-Series made its debut.

The S-Series was manufactured from late 1955 until mid-1957. The design was apparently refined from the R-Series although they had a squarer appearance, partially as a result of the headlights which were mounted high on the fenders rather than within the confines of the radiator grille as previously. The windshield was redesigned to increase visibility. Different payload options continued and a choice of interiors was available. IHC considered 1957 to be its 50th year in truck manufacture and brought out special models to mark the occasion. The range of trucks which had been significantly redesigned were designated A-Series for Anniversary. The styling was modern and angular and the trucks came with a choice of bed styles: there was the custom pickup and pickups which were effectively fleetside and stepside models. The fleetside-type bed was constructed using the rear fenders of the IHC Travelall station wagon. For 1959, the range of trucks was designated the B-Series which was the previous year's A-Series face-lifted. Design features of the B-Series included quad headlamps and a chromed car-like grille. This range was carried over into 1960, the only major change being that a V8 engine was now standard equipment.

International Harvester hit the headlines in 1961 with the introduction of the Scout, one of the first sport utilities. It was a small, boxy pickup with rounded-off corners and a truck cab designed to seat three. The tailgate hinged downwards and the

International Harvester, like most other manufacturers, offered its light trucks with a choice of rear bodies. One option was to simply buy a chassis-cab, i.e. a vehicle with no rear body fitted, so that a specialist rear body could be fitted. This thirties D-Series International has the maker's logo above the grille but was supplied for conversion into a light tanker. It is a D-15 one-tonner with an 130-inch (330-cm) wheelbase.

cab roof was removable. The grille was rectangular and single circular headlights were positioned on either side of it. The Scout was available in both two- and four-wheel-drive versions, rated as a quarter-ton and was known as the Model 80. It was powered by a four-cylinder engine and the whole machine was constructed around a 100-inch (254-cm) wheelbase. The machine was a success and in excess of 28,000 were sold in 1961. The Model C pickups were upgraded versions of the Model B-Series of which there was a comprehensive range; C-100/C-102 models were half-tonners on a 119-inch (302-cm) wheelbase; C-110/C-112 trucks were three-quarter-tonners on 115-, 119-, 122-, 131- and 140-inch (292-, 302-, 310-, 333- and 356-cm) wheelbases; C-120/C-122 were one-tonners based on 115-, 119-, 122-, 131- and 140-inch wheelbases. The C-130/C-132 was a one-ton chassis-cab with 122-, 131-, 134- and 140-inch (310-, 333-, 340- and 356-cm) wheelbases.

Both the Model 80 Scout and the C-Series pickups continued for 1962 with minimal changes. Roll-up windows were an option on the Scout and the doors could be removed for off-road use.

Folded flat windshield and vinyl roof options were also available. It was a similar story for 1963 and 1964 for the Scout although the pickup line was restyled.

The Scout was partially redesigned and upgraded for 1965, a new grille, new hood emblems and a permanently fixed leak-free windshield being among the upgrades. The windshield wipers, pedals and numerous interior details were also improved. The Scout was still available in both 4x2 and 4x4 forms although 82 per cent of Scouts sold in 1965 were 4x4 models. The company also discovered that half the Scout buyers had never owned an International before and that trade-ins against Scouts included a large proportion of both sportscars and station wagons. These facts influenced International who marketed Scouts with more luxurious interiors and for 1966 offered in-line six-cylinder engines and, later in the same year, V8 options. For 1967 the Scout was marketed with three different interior and exterior trim levels, Utility, Custom and Sportop. The Utility models featured bench seats and painted bumpers. The Custom models had a number of interior comforts including bucket seats, arm rests, sun visors and vinyl trim, as well as chromed fenders and hub caps. The Sportop featured a slanted back roof, hence its name, and had bucket seats and other luxury trims as well as chrome

mouldings and trims in addition to the fenders. The range of colours reflected the sport utility lines and included Aspen Green, Bahamas Blue and Tahitian Yellow. Alongside these models the production of conventional trucks continued as did production of Travelalls and crew cabs in both two- and four-wheel-drive forms. Little changed for 1968 and there were limited-edition Scout models for the 1969–70 production run. The Scout Aristocrat included upgrades such as two-tone paint and wide chrome wheels. IHC's line of conventional pickup trucks was redesigned for 1969 and were given wide, flat hoods and slab-sided fenders, a design reminiscent of the still successful Scout models. Its success continued despite the introduction by rival manufacturers of competing vehicles in the sport utility class. An eight-track stereo system was an option for the Scout models.

More changes came for 1971 with the introduction of the Scout II, alongside the Scout, and the conventional light trucks. The new Scout, introduced in the spring of 1971, was redesigned and incorporated power brakes, power steering, air-conditioning, automatic transmission and a V8. The body was longer and lower than the previous model and sales exceeded 30,000 in the first year of production. The six-cylinder-powered Series D trucks continued with minor upgrades. For 1972 the Scout was discontinued while the Scout II continued, upgraded in small details such as the radiator grille. The front end of the Scout II was redesigned again for 1973, as was that fitted to the Series 1010, 1110 and 1210 range of trucks. By this time IHC was America's fifth-largest truck maker behind Chevrolet, Ford, Dodge and GMC in that order.

The Scout went into 1974 unchanged while the pickups were given new designations, becoming the 100 and 200 models for the half- and three-quarter-tonners respectively. The pickups remained in production until 1975 when the line was discontinued, as was the Travelall. The Scout II remained in production, however, with few changes beyond a slightly different range of optional V8 engines. The production run of the Scout II lasted until 1980 after which the company concentrated on the heavy truck market. The last years of the Scouts saw the models increasingly aimed at the sport utility market although there were pickups made. The pickups included models such as the Scout II Terra Compact Sport Pickup.

OPPOSITE
International Harvester introduced its range of 4x4 pickups in the early fifties and manufactured them for many years. This one is a 1956 S-120 model that still earns its keep in South Dakota.

LEFT
The International Harvester emblem is prominently displayed on the hood.

OPPOSITE AND LEFT
The International Scout was one of
the first sport utility vehicles (SUVs),
although the term was yet to be
conceived when the Scout was
introduced in 1961. This 1967 4x4
model is owned by John Marchant
and is based around a 100-inch
(254-cm) wheelbase. Other variants
were available with different types of
roofs.

Chapter 6
JEEP

Willys-Overland diversified from its famous wartime Jeep into the production of working trucks, including the 1-ton range of 4x4 models and the later J-20 range.

The history of the various vehicles to have carried the Jeep name is considerably shorter than those of many of the other American manufacturers. The reason for this is that, although Jeep is a brand and registered trade-name, it has been produced by a variety of manufacturers. The Jeep itself originated out of the U.S. Army quarter-ton 4x4 reconnaissance truck and prototypes for it were prepared by Willys-Overland, Bantam and Ford. While the original design can be mostly attributed to Bantam and much of the wartime mass-production to Ford, it was Willys who produced the final but one design of quarter-ton 4x4 and the one that the U.S. Army adopted with a few modifications – the Willys MA and subsequently the Willys MB. At the finish of World War II, Willys-Overland began to develop the Jeep as a useful peacetime tool for farmers and others working on unpaved roads. In many ways the immediate post-war Jeeps pioneered the mass market for four-wheel-drive vehicles. Willys-Overland produced the CJ2A, a civilianized version of the wartime MB with a number of detail changes to the transmission but also with features to make it more suited to civilian use. As well as a variety of paint colours the company offered Jeeps with fold-down rear tailgates, power take-off (PTO) points and implement attachments. The CJ2A gave way to the CJ3A in 1950

In June 1940 the U.S. Quartermaster Corps issued a specification for a lightweight vehicle capable of carrying men and equipment across rough terrain and invited manufacturers to build prototypes and submit them for testing. Two manufacturers showed sufficient interest, namely Willys-Overland and American Bantam, both of which were in some financial difficulty at the

time. The Willys prototype was late in arriving and Bantam received a contract for 70 vehicles after its machine – the Bantam BRC – had been thoroughly tested at Camp Holabird, in Maryland. Both Ford and Willys were given copies of blueprints for the Bantam machine which suggested to some that the army was doubting Bantam's ability to build and supply its 4x4 in the numbers required. Further contracts were issued requesting vehicles from Ford and Willys who subsequently submitted their prototypes, the Pygmy and the Quad respectively. All three

OPPOSITE
Jeep introduced a line of light duty 4x4 trucks immediately after World War II. The model was a success and the Jeep truck line endured for many years. Upgrades over the years included a slight redesign of the grille from the flat one seen on this 1948 model.

LEFT
This California gardener's hard-worked Willys truck is the later version with the redesigned grille. It is much more peaked than the early models but the basic truck is the same with the utility rear body and basic fenders.

companies' machines had the early Jeep 'look' and further tests revealed that all three machines possessed both strengths and weaknesses in equal measure. Ford submitted a redesigned prototype, the Ford GP, as did Willys – the MA. It was the Willys MA, after further strenuous evaluation tests, that appeared superior overall and in July 1941 Willys was given a contract for 16,000 revised MA models which were referred to as the MB, and the Bantam BRC and Ford GP quickly faded into the background. Ford, who had a massive manufacturing capability, accepted a contract in November 1941 to manufacture the Willys MB to Willys specifications and the Ford-built examples were known as GPWs. So the legend of the Jeep was born and in every theatre of war, from the mud of the Belgian Ardennes to the jungles of Burma and the sands of Iwo Jima, the Jeep endeared itself to the allied armies. Fighting machine, ambulance, message carrier, mechanical mule, recreational vehicle – the Willys Jeep encompassed all and more. It was the transport of all ranks from privates to generals on all types of terrain. At the end of the war General Eisenhower commented that the Jeep was as important a tool in the struggle to win the war as the amphibious truck, the Douglas DC3 aircraft and the bulldozer. By the end of the war Willys had built 358,489 MB Jeeps and Ford had built 277,896 GPWs.

The MB/GPW in its final form had two differential-equipped axles mounted to the Jeep's channel section steel chassis by semi-elliptical springs. The gearbox featured three forward and one reverse gear with a high and low ratio selected by means of an additional gear lever. A third lever enabled selection of two- or four-wheel-drive to be made though the low ratio gears could only be used in four-wheel-drive. The basic steel body tub was bolted to the chassis, the hood was collapsible, and the windscreen could be folded forward onto the bonnet to present a lower silhouette. The interior was extremely basic and contained little more than seats with canvas-covered cushions to provide seating for four people, two in the front on individual seats and the others on the rear bench seat. The exterior of the vehicle had brackets to carry

an axe and spade, a jerrican, and a spare wheel and tyre. It has been jokingly suggested that Jeep is an acronym for 'Just enough essential parts'. A number of Jeep variants were considered and built as prototypes, including a six-wheeled Jeep and a four-wheel-steering Jeep, while other variants actually went into production. The best known of these variants was an amphibious Jeep nicknamed the Seep and many Jeeps were modified for specific tasks such as transporting stretcher-borne casualties or for air transportation. Even before the end of World War II Willys-

Four-wheel-drive vehicles have long been popular for commercial applications. This Forward Control Willys truck (OPPOSITE LEFT) was a way of increasing a Jeep's load area while retaining a relatively short wheelbase. As the badge (OPPOSITE RIGHT) shows, this truck is the longer wheelbase FC-170 model and is equipped with a stakebed body (LEFT) which is particularly suited to agricultural use.

Overland knew it was on to a good thing with the Jeep – its product and its trade-mark – that had served the Allies so faithfully in every theatre of operations and realized that a civilian Jeep would be just as versatile for all sorts of agricultural and commercial tasks. So the CJ2A was born and the first models rolled off the Toledo line alongside the last MB Jeeps for the U.S. Army. Changes were minimal for 1945 CJ2A models but included a rear tailgate to facilitate easier loading, a side-mounted spare wheel, and the maker's name pressed into more of the panels. The CJ2A featured the same four-cylinder L-head Go-Devil engine and 80-inch (203-cm) wheelbase. To make the vehicle more useful for farming and industrial applications it was possible to specify either front, rear or centre power take-off as an extra cost option. One refinement that soon followed was the supply of Jeeps with larger headlights made possible by reducing the number of pressed apertures in the grille from nine to seven.

Willys-Overland, who had had the foresight to register Jeep as its trade-mark, began to prepare for the production of civilian Jeeps to be tagged CJs. Initially the Jeep CJs were marketed for agricultural purposes being equipped with power take-offs and agricultural drawbars. They were promoted through a variety of farming applications such as for towing ploughs and as disc rotators. Other early variants were fitted with firefighting equipment made by the Howe Fire Apparatus Corporation of Anderson, Indiana. The first post-war Jeep, the CJ2A, appeared superficially to be simply a Jeep of a different colour to the military model although, under the skin, it in fact featured revised transmission, axles and differential ratios. More obvious alterations were the inclusion of a hinged tailgate and relocation of the spare wheel to the vehicle's side. There were numerous detail improvements including bigger headlights and a relocated fuel cap. The engine was only slightly upgraded from the MB. Production of the CJ2A lasted until 1949 by which time there had been 214,202 produced. This production run overlapped with the second of the CJs – the CJ3A. This Jeep went into mass-production in 1948 and continued until 1953. The main differences between the CJ2A and CJ3A were a further strengthened transmission and transfer case and a one-piece windshield. In 1953 the CJ3B was introduced with a noticeably different silhouette because of a higher bonnet line. This change was necessary in order for Willys to fit a new engine. The Hurricane F-head four-cylinder was a taller engine that displaced the same 134 cubic inches (2196cc) but produced more horsepower. The CJ3B was to remain in production until the sixties and a total of 155,494 were constructed. This model CJ was destined to live on until the present day through a series of licensing agreements that meant it would be constructed in European, Indian and Japanese factories. Kaiser-Frazer and Willys-Overland merged in 1953 and the resulting company was known as Kaiser-Jeep.

Another Jeep was built from 1954 onwards for the military – the M38A1 – and a civilian version was introduced the following year and tagged the CJ5. It was slightly larger than the 'flat-fenders' that had come before it as its wheelbase was one inch longer but as the nickname of the early models perhaps indicates, its fenders were not flat. The bonnet and fenders, or wings, were noticeably curved although the vehicle was still basic and featured a flat-sided design and a grille that was recognizably Jeep. Another model appeared at the same time, the CJ6, which as a simply longer version of the CJ5 aimed at giving commercial users

OPPOSITE
By 1981 Jeeps were produced by AMC – American Motors Corporation – who had continued the Jeep tradition of offering four-wheel-drive pickups. This 1981 model has stepside rear fenders although a townside option with smooth sides was available. The model was designated J-10 and was known as the Honcho. The J-10 featured a mixture of pickup and four-wheel-drive parts such as the drop-down tailgate, stepside fenders, Jeep tail-lights and 4x4 badging (LEFT).

Jeep Honcho trucks were available in two wheelbases: 119 and 131 inches (302 and 333cm) and two payloads of half and three-quarters of a ton. This is the 119-inch half-ton variant.

a much larger load area. It had a 101-inch (257-cm) wheelbase compared to the 81-inch (206-cm) CJ5.

It is generally acknowledged that the CJ5 is the model that helped to popularize recreational off-road driving, especially during the seventies when the fact was emphasized that Jeeps could be 'fun' vehicles. The CJ5 was a popular model in the customers' eyes and ensured a healthy profit for its

manufacturers although the company's car production side was unprofitable and was abandoned to allow it to concentrate on Jeep production. A spin-off of this policy was the introduction of special Jeeps such as the forward control models and limited-edition vehicles such as the 1961 Tuxedo Park. This was a CJ5 dressed up with chrome hinges, mirror supports and bumper, custom wheels and whitewall tyres and custom hood. This model, intended for golf courses and hotels, remained in production until 1966 in slightly upgraded form with different paint options and better seats.

The forward control type of light truck was frequently bodied as a walk-in-type panel van. The thinking behind these machines was that, by putting the cab over the front axle and engine, a larger load bed would be created while at the same time retaining a relatively short wheelbase. Such vehicles were built, among others, by Jeep. The 4x4 Jeep models were first introduced in 1957 and remained in production for seven years. There were two models, the FC-150 and FC-170. The FC prefix clearly stands for forward control and the numerical designation refers to the dimensions of the wheelbase. The FC-150 was based around the 81-inch wheelbase of the CJ5 then in production while the FC-170 was based on a 103.5-inch (263-cm) wheelbase chassis. The short wheelbase model had a four-cylinder engine and the longer one a six. The remainder of the machines were similar, both utilizing leaf-sprung axles, drum brakes, two-speed transfer boxes and three-speed gearboxes.

Another series was based around the same chassis, mechanical parts and front sheetmetal as the Willys sedan deliveries, the 4-75 models. These were available in two- and four-wheel-drive variants and with different payloads. The designation changed from time to time and by 1957 the one-ton four-cylinder-engined 4x4 pickup was tagged the F4-134. It was of a general design that Willys-Overland had introduced in the immediate post-war years to capitalize on the success of the Willys Jeep by offering a commercial variant. This was a longer wheelbase pickup with a closed cab but had frontal styling that resembled the Willys MB. The first of these were offered in 1947 and the model survived the acquisition of Willys-Overland by the Kaiser Manufacturing Company and with various minor upgrades and styling changes would run until the sixties. After 1962 the trucks were redesigned with a rather more modern appearance but both models were produced in parallel for a few years. Another commercial Jeep introduced in the late fifties was the CJ6, a long wheelbase version of the CJ5 sharing front and rear sheetmetal, axles, engine and transmission, but which simply had an extra 20 inches (51cm) in the wheelbase.

By 1963 the Jeep range included CJ3B and CJ5 Jeeps with the CJ6 still available as the longer wheelbase commercial variant, the F-134 model pickups, the FC-Series of forward control pickups and the newer, more modern-looking J Series available in two- and four-wheel-drive combinations with payloads of half, three-quarters and one ton (1,016kg) and a choice of three wheelbases. This range continued for 1964, 1965 and 1966 with only minor changes. The CJ3B and DJ3A models were discontinued in 1967. For the remainder of the sixties, Jeep continued to develop its range, the CJ5 and CJ6 models continued in production and other models such as the Jeepster Commando and Wagoneer continued to be produced. Jeep aimed its products at both the commercial as well as the recreational user; the pickups were destined to be sold to farmers and similar while machines such as the Commando and Wagoneer were aimed at the embryonic sport utility market. Camper options also appealed to the latter market. In 1970 Kaiser-Jeep was purchased by American Motors Corporation (AMC) for approximately $70 million. AMC changed the name of the Jeep-producing organization to the Jeep Corporation but made only minor changes to the Jeep models initially. A special edition Jeepster – the Hurst Jeepster Special – was marketed in 1971. More radical design changes were made for 1972 with a new range of engines for the CJ range which necessitated lengthening the wheelbase of both the CJ5 and CJ6 models to accommodate them. The extra length was incorporated into the front fenders so that the appearance remained almost the same overall. Mechanically, a new rear axle and transfer case was adopted as was a larger diameter clutch and redesigned pedals. The front-end sheetmetal of the Commando was redesigned and the J-Series trucks were available with a greater payload on the 120-inch (305-cm) wheelbase chassis.

Design changes were continued for 1973 when the J-series trucks received a wider tailgate and numerous detail improvements. They were also offered with the option of Quadra-Trac transmission, a full-time 4x4 system. The CJ models received detail upgrades and the Renegade trim package was first offered. There were no great changes for 1974 and 1975 but new for 1976 was the CJ7 with a 93.5-inch (237-cm) wheelbase. It was in many ways a longer wheelbase variant of the CJ5 and was seen as one of the most exciting developments in the 4x4 market

for several years. Also new for 1976 was the Honcho package for the ongoing J-10 pickup in short wheelbase form. Available in a choice of six base colours, the Honcho was essentially a dress-up package for the workaday J-10. It included wide 15-inch (38-cm) wheels and tyres, gold pinstriping, rear step bumpers and a denim interior. In this year Jeep sold more than 12,000 J-10 and J-20 pickups. The Honcho package remained available for 1977, 1978 and 1979.

Into the eighties and the Honcho package was still available for J-10s as one of a range of trim levels and options that also included the Custom, the top-of-the-range Laredo, the Sportside, and the Honcho Sportside packages and options for automatic transmission and a V8 engine. New for 1981 was the CJ8 Scrambler, a sport utility vehicle that featured CJ7-type front sheetmetal and a rear load bed on a 104-inch (264-cm) wheelbase chassis. Like the J-10, this 4x4 was powered by an ohv in-line six-cylinder engine of 258-cubic inch (4228-cc) displacement. Little changed for 1982 and the company was making a loss apart from there being specialty option packages on offer. In this form the range of CJ and J-Series Jeep products continued almost unchanged until the end of CJ production in January 1986. It was subsequently replaced by the YJ Wrangler but also new that year was the Jeep Commanche pickup which shared much of its front sheetmetal with the new style Jeep Cherokee XJ station wagon. The Commanche, a down-sized truck designed to compete head-on with the Japanese imports was available in both 4x2 and 4x4 forms on a 120-inch (305-cm) wheelbase chassis. It was powered by an in-line four-cylinder engine and a turbo diesel engine was listed as an option.

LEFT
Barry Redman's 1947 CJ2A Willys Jeep. The first civilian Jeeps made in post-war years clearly show their wartime origins but incorporated features such as bottom-hinged tailgates (RIGHT) to facilitate their use on farms and for similar applications.

Chapter 7
OTHER MANUFACTURERS

Plymouth and Studebaker produced such famous pickups as the Plymouth Trail Duster and the Studebaker Champ. Pontiac's output was somewhat smaller but it is a no less famous name.

OPPOSITE
Tommy Jarrett's V8-powered 1947 M5 Studebaker street-rod pickup. It now has a scratch-built chassis and a Rover V8 engine but was originally bought in South Africa in a derelict condition after being damaged in an accident.

While Pontiac's production of light trucks was confined to a very few vehicles in the mid-twenties and a number of sedan deliveries based on its current car range of the late forties and early fifties, other manufacturers such as Plymouth and Studebaker produced light trucks in considerable numbers.

PLYMOUTH

Plymouth commercial vehicles were offered between 1935 and 1942 alongside Dodge trucks, both companies being part of the Chrysler group. Plymouth was the low-cost brand and the same strategy was employed with pickups where dealers with joint Chrysler-Dodge franchises were offered an opportunity for increased sales. The first arrivals were 'commercial cars' – passenger cars produced in sedan delivery formats. Production was small in number but was considered sufficiently worthwhile for the company to increase the range from 1938 onwards, which included the PT57 pickup. For 1939 the range included the PT81, powered by an in-line six-cylinder engine driving through a three-speed transmission. Slightly more than 6,000 of these trucks were

produced. By 1940 the company was offering the PT105 pickup which closely resembled the Dodge trucks of the time. It was powered by an in-line six-cylinder engine of 201.3-cubic inch (3299-cc) displacement that produced 79 bhp @ 3,000 rpm. The truck was based on an 116-inch (295-cm) wheelbase chassis. The slightly upgraded models for 1941 became the PT125 series and were the last trucks from Plymouth for 33 years.

Production of Plymouth light utility vehicles was not resumed until 1974 when the company released the Trail Duster onto the sport utility market. The Trail Duster was a slab-sided vehicle, typical of trucks of the time, and was available as an open machine with either a soft top or a fibreglass top. The 1974 model was available as a 106-inch (269-cm) wheelbase 4x4 powered by a V8 with automatic transfer with a number of shift positions for off-road use. A 4x2 variant of the Trail Duster was introduced in 1975 and featured independent front suspension in place of the driven live axle. The 4x4 model continued as for the previous year although minor trim and colour changes were made and a sport package was offered. It was the same story for 1976 but the

ABOVE
The Studebaker brand name appears on the hood above the slightly modified radiator grille. The whole truck is finished in Peugeot Red.

OPPOSITE
The Studebaker series of pickup trucks had been extensively redesigned by 1951 when this 2R-Series model was made.

vehicles received a face-lift for 1977. The grille was redesigned with horizontal bars and vertical signal lights while the Plymouth badge shifted from the centre of the grille to the face of the hood. The standard engine was the in-line six-cylinder although the V8 was an option.

The models were left untouched for 1978 after the 1977 redesign but new options were offered such as different seats, tinted glass, tilt steering column and CB radio integrated with AM/FM stereo. New for 1979 was the Plymouth Arrow, a down-sized mini-pickup made for Plymouth by Mitsubishi in Japan. The Arrow was powered by an in-line four-cylinder engine of 122-cubic inch (1999-cc) displacement. A sport package for the same truck was also offered that included bucket seats, extra dashboard gauges, spoked sport wheels and decals. Alongside this mini-truck the Trail Duster continued with a redesigned grille and three-speed manual transmission as standard.

STUDEBAKER

Studebaker's involvement with light trucks goes back long before the advent of the motor vehicle to 1852 when Henry and Clem Studebaker had their blacksmith's shop in South Bend, Indiana, making wagons for local farmers. From these humble beginnings evolved a reputable manufacturing operation producing horse-drawn vehicles which by 1876 had grown to be a large concern. After experimenting with some early automobile designs and electric propulsion, around the turn of the century, they finally introduced an internal combustion engined-automobile in 1902. Studebaker cooperated with other fledgeling manufacturers in its locale, including the EMF Co. and Flanders, and by 1914 was established enough to introduce a proper light commercial vehicle of its own, the three-quarter-ton Model Three Delivery Car. This truck was available in two forms, as a panel or an express delivery, i.e. as van or pickup. These machines were powered by an in-line four-cylinder engine of 192.4-cubic inch (3153-cc) displacement. It achieved this with a bore and stroke of 3.5 x 5 inches (8.9 x 12.7cm) and produced 30 hp. These vehicles remained in production for several years until 1918 when Studebaker discontinued all motorized commercial vehicles. Production was not resumed until 1927. In this year a new commercial vehicle was produced which continued until 1931 when it was abandoned.

In 1937 Studebaker introduced another commercial vehicle: sales were good and the company remained in the pickup business until the closure of its Indiana plant in 1963. The 1937 model was the coupé express which sourced most of its front sheetmetal from the Studebaker 5A Dictator car of the time. The truck was based around an 116-inch (295-cm) wheelbase and power came from an in-line six-cylinder L-head engine of 217.8-cubic inch (3569-cc) displacement. For 1938 the pickup was also based on the concurrently produced car and so featured the same front-end bodywork. Specialist machines were offered, including large capacity furniture vans, fire trucks and similar. Again, for 1939, the pickup shared its front end with the car line leading to the truck being redesigned in line with the new range of cars.

A whole new line of Studebaker pickups was introduced for the 1941 model year and tagged the M-Series. They all used a common cab and front end, both of which were unique to the

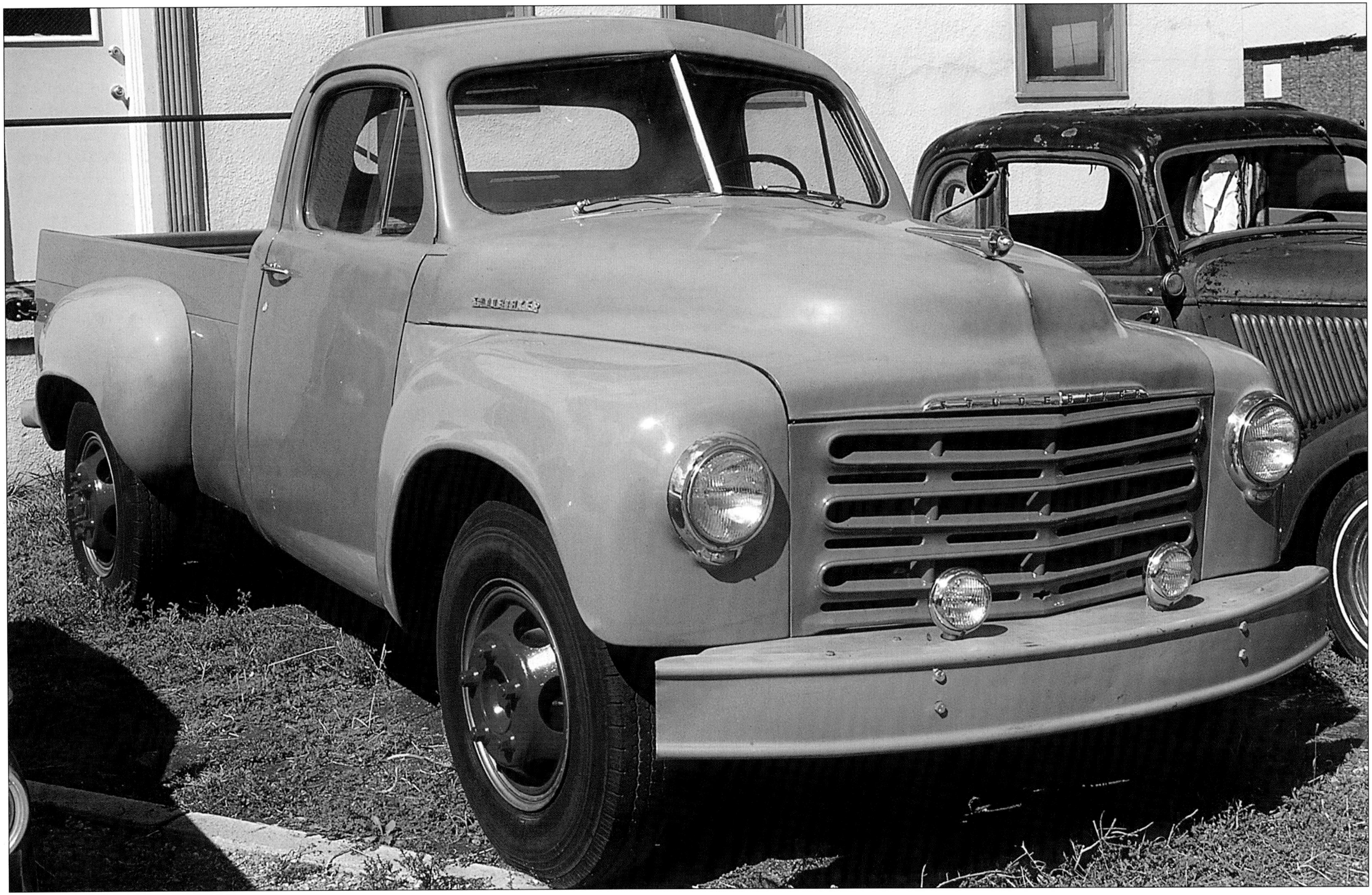

ABOVE
The Studebaker Champ pickup was the company's last body design before production ended in the early sixties. It contrasts markedly with the early fifties models with stepside rear bodies (OPPOSITE).

truck line. The truck was built with economic priorities in mind so that the running boards were interchangeable from side to side to minimize production costs and the front and rear fenders were interchangeable on a give side. An I-beam front suspension system was used on the 113-inch (287-cm) wheelbase truck that was powered by an in-line six-cylinder engine. The company sold more than 8,000 in the first year of production.

Like other U.S. auto makers, the advent of World War II interrupted Studebaker's civilian vehicle production and the production capacity was turned to the war effort. Studebaker assembled almost 200,000 US6 2½-ton 6x4 and 6x6 trucks. Half of these went to the U.S.S.R. as lend lease equipment. The GAZ plant in Gorky, Russia, produced a close copy of this truck in the post-war years. Studebaker also produced Wright Cyclone Flying Fortress engines and in excess of 15,000 Weasels, a light, fully-tracked military vehicle. This machine was designed by Studebaker's engineers and can be regarded as one of the pioneers of the light tracked vehicle and ATV. Studebaker was, with other manufacturers, to produce trucks for essential civilian use

towards the end of the war. Following the cessation of hostilities, the company reintroduced its pre-war M-series trucks as 1946 and subsequently 1947 and 1948 models. In 1947 the company produced more than 67,000 trucks, a figure which exceeded the total of all the trucks the company had produced pre-war.

A new line of trucks which appeared in 1949 was dubbed the 2R-Series. There were half-ton 2R5 models, three-quarter-ton 2R10 models and one-ton 2R15 models. These were of a completely new design by Robert Bourke and had no sheetmetal in common with Studebaker's car range. The 2R5 and 2R10 models used 112- and 122-inch (284- and 310-cm) wheelbases respectively and were powered by six-cylinder engines. The trucks were assembled in the wartime plant that Studebaker had used to assemble the aero engines. The plant had been built by the U.S. government for war production and Studebaker bought it afterwards and prepared it for truck production. The initial post-war sales boom did not last long and before the end of the decade trucks were slow to move from dealers' showroom floors. To combat this, Studebaker instituted a year model registration procedure that meant a 1949-built truck could be registered as a 1950 model. This was not dissimilar to the system employed by IHC and meant that the smaller manufacturers could avoid competing each autumn with new lines from the larger manufacturers. The 1949 2R model sold well, however, and few changes were consequently made for 1950, 1951, 1952 or the final year of 2R production 1953. The trucks were redesignated the 3R-Series for 1954 and given a minor face-lift. Much of the sheetmetal remained the same although the grille was redesigned and a curved one-piece windshield superseded the two-piece item used until then. For 1955, styling changes were kept to a minimum but numerous upgrades were made to the power train of the trucks. Because of these changes, including the use of an overhead valve V8 in some models, the trucks were again redesignated, this time as the E-Series. There were E5 and E7 half-ton trucks and E10 and E12 three-quarter tonners, the E7 and E12 models being the V8-powered versions. The V8 models proved popular and helped Studebaker to achieve a good sales total for the year.

In October 1954 Studebaker merged with Packard but it was not really to either company's advantage and by 1956 Studebaker had lost money for every year of the association. This meant that cash was no longer available for the complete redesign of the truck range. A new name – Transtar – and a minor redesign was all that could be done but the name proved popular. Sales were not what they had been and Studebaker truck production was moved back to the main Studebaker plant and the wartime plant leased to another company. The company began to make annual changes to its model line and alongside the Transtar introduced a basic pickup known as the Scotsman. It was the lowest priced pickup on sale in the United States in 1958. This year was a difficult one for Studebaker until it introduced the Lark passenger car which sold well and reversed the company's fortunes. There were Lark trucks but there were Lark panel vans and Lark styling would later appear on the Studebaker Champ pickups. The Champ appeared in 1960 in both 4x2 and 4x4 forms, as had the Transtar, alongside which the Champ was manufactured and sold. Studebaker trucks were manufactured until 1963/64.

Chapter 8
AROUND THE WORLD

The pickup truck's appeal is not just an American phenomenon - pickups are used the world over.

In the United States, in 1956, Dodge was building the Power Wagon, and Jeep the CJ3B, CJ5, CJ6 and a four-wheel-drive pickup truck, while in Great Britain, the 86- and 107-inch (218- and 272-cm) Series I Land Rovers were beginning to appear and the value of both pickups and four-wheel-drive vehicles to post-war commercial users was becoming clearly apparent. Toyota got in on the act soon after and the rest, as they say, is history.

Two things are particularly common in the manufacture of commercial vehicles, namely building under licence and the marketing of machines in different countries under different names. The phenomenon of licence-building has continued from the immediate post-war years when Willys licensed other companies on other continents to build its products. Vehicles are supplied by the original manufacturer as CKD (completely knocked down) kits and assembled elsewhere or are produced entirely locally. The latter option often keeps earlier models in production where function is more important than fashion in the more style-conscious markets of Europe and North America. Marketing vehicles under different names occurs for several

LEFT
Winston Churchill, the former British
prime minister, approved of the Land
Rover as a workhorse because
exports of early models considerably
helped Britain's balance of payments
in the years immediately following
World War II. The famous politician
is seen here with a short wheelbase
Series I Land Rover.

reasons: sometimes a different model name is perceived as being more in tune with a particular market or, in the global case of multinational motor manufacturers, the same vehicle is produced not only by different plants but nominally different companies. An example of this is General Motors, which produces Isuzu, Vauxhall, Opel and Holden pickups around the world.

The Land Rover is a completely British, light commercial vehicle, produced in numerous pickup variants. The roots of the Land Rover lie undeniably in the wartime Willys Jeep when Maurice Wilks, chief engineer of the Rover Company, obtained an army surplus Jeep for use on his Anglesey estate. In the early post-war years Rover, who had a reputation for building quality

motor cars, was in a difficult position because of the shortage of steel and the fact that it was allocated to companies producing goods for export destined to ease Britain's balance of payments deficit. Rover had never been a serious exporter of its cars beyond some sales to Britain's colonies. During the war years its Coventry factory had been blitzed and the company moved out to Solihull where it produced items for the Air Ministry. After seriously investigating the possibilities of a small aluminium-bodied car, Maurice Wilks and his brother Spencer, also a Rover employee, considered the viability of a small utility vehicle with an aluminium body (which unlike steel was not rationed), and four-wheel-drive. The intention was that the machine, specifically

OPPOSITE
From the time of the Series I
onwards, there have been long
wheelbase variants of the utilitarian
Land Rovers. This is a Series I model
fitted with a truck cab and a cover
over the pickup load bed.

intended for agricultural use, would be a stopgap until sufficient steel became available for the company to return to building luxury cars. The Wilks brothers delegated much of the design work to Robert Boyle and other employees in the drawing office. Rover also purchased two army surplus Jeeps on which to base its design. The designers were set other criteria: the vehicle was to utilize existing Rover components as far as possible to avoid expensive tooling costs and the panels would be flat or worked by hand. These first Land Rovers had a tractor-like centre steering-wheel to enable it to be used as either left- or right-hand drive. Because a conventional chassis would have required expensive tooling the engineer, Olaf Poppe, devised a jig on which four strips of flat steel could be welded together to form a box section chassis. The first prototype featured a Jeep chassis, an existing Rover car rear axle and springs, a Rover car engine and production saloon gearbox cleverly mated to a two-speed transfer box and a Jeep-like body. It was seen to have potential and an improved version was given the go-ahead in that 50 should be built for further evaluation. A larger and more powerful but still extant Rover car engine was fitted and the centre steering-wheel was dropped. In very nearly this form the 80-inch (203-cm) wheelbase vehicle was shown to the public at the 1948 Amsterdam motor show. Orders flowed in, especially when early Land Rovers were displayed at agricultural shows around Britain, and the company began to look seriously at export markets. An indication of its potential was that, by October 1948, there were Land Rover dealerships in 68 countries.

Significant changes were again made to the Land Rover for 1956 when two wheelbases, 88 and 109 inches (224 and 277cm), were available which were referred to by Rover as Regular and Long models. By 1958 Rover had produced in excess of 200,000 Land Rovers and it became obvious that the model was more than a mere stopgap. It is estimated that more than 70 per cent of Land Rovers produced went for export. Rover once again sought to improve its product. In April 1958 it introduced what was termed the Series II Land Rover and after this the early models were referred to as Series Is although they are commonly described by their wheelbase lengths, '80s' and '86s', and this practice endured into later models which are described as '88s' and '109s'.

The Series II featured a redesigned body that was 1.5 inches (4cm) wider than its predecessors and featured other minor improvements which included more up to date door hinges and bonnet latches. Soon after its introduction, the Series II was fitted with a larger engine that displaced 139 cubic inches (2286cc). Wider track axles were fitted underneath and better suspension components gave a more comfortable ride. The idea was to update the Land Rover without changing it significantly and truck cab pickups, hardtop vans, station wagons and models with canvas tilts remained available in both wheelbase lengths. A further upgraded model appeared in 1961, the Series IIa. Many of the changes were minimal but one of particular note was the improved diesel engine which now also displaced 139 cubic inches (2286cc). Great Britain was not the only place where legislation affected vehicle sales and a front end redesign was necessary to ensure that it conformed to the laws of certain American states relating to headlights. These were moved from the radiator grille panel into the fronts of the wings. In April 1966 the 500,000th Land Rover was manufactured which remained little changed until September 1971 when the Series III was announced. By March 1967 Rover had become part of the British Leyland Motor Corporation. While sales were profitable, the corporation as a whole was not and this at times had serious ramifications for the Land Rover.

The Series III Land Rover was possibly a demonstration that management was keeping up with the times; many of the changes were cosmetic and perceived as important only to keep Land Rover vehicles seemingly up to date. There were a number of mechanical upgrades of which the most noticeable was the new all-synchromesh gearbox. This accompanied uprated brakes, clutch, and rear axle on 109-inch models. The cosmetic changes included features such as a moulded plastic radiator grille and new door hinges while inside, the dashboard was padded and relocated in front of the driver and a number of the electrical function switches were placed on a stalk on the steering column.

When investment in the Land Rover was perceived as more secure, a V8 variant was planned. The Range Rover and numerous cars used the aluminium V8 originally derived from Buick as a 215-cubic inch (3523-cc) iron engine. The first V8 model was referred to as the Stage One and was only available in

The Minor pickup was made in England by the Morris Company, initially independently and later as part of the British Motor Corporation (BMC) conglomerate. The Minor was also available as a light van and as a chassis-cab for fitment of specialist bodies. This one was made in 1969 and is powered by an in-line four-cylinder of 67 cubic inches (1098cc) displacement. Through the production run, several capacities were marketed but all were in the region of a quarter of a ton.

the long wheelbase models. County models, with more luxurious interiors and special paint schemes, and high capacity pickups, were introduced at this time but the company was already looking beyond this to the new models, the Ninety and the One Ten. So entrenched had the terms 88 and 109 become that the new models were officially designated Ninety and One Ten referring to wheelbases of 90 and 110 inches respectively. In fact, the wheelbase of the Ninety measured almost 93 inches (236cm) though the One Ten actually measured 110 inches (279cm).

Unlike the other redesigns, which were relatively minor, the Ninety and One Ten were different from all that had gone before but for the fact that they still looked like Land Rovers. The One Ten was unveiled at the Geneva Motor Show in March 1983 and featured the coil spring suspension set-up that had been used on the Range Rover since 1970.

Another famous British pickup was the Morris Minor, produced as a light truck variant of the Morris Minor saloon designed by Alec Issigonis. The pickup was made between 1953

Almost since its inception the Land Rover has been offered in two wheelbases and with a variety of body styles. This is a Land Rover 90 pickup at work in a typical environment. The Defender 90 is the current short wheelbase model and the numerical designation approximates to the length of the wheelbase in inches.

and 1971 in numerous forms and was sequentially updated alongside the saloon models in terms of engine size and styling changes such as the move away from a two-piece to a one-piece curved windshield. There were also pickup variants of the tiny Mini – also designed by Alec Issigonis – but produced in small numbers compared to Mini saloons.

It was however elsewhere in the world, most notably Japan, that real innovation was appearing in the production of light commercial vehicles. Mitsubishi, Nissan and Toyota all began producing light commercials. In the early fifties, Mitsubishi Heavy Industries Limited entered into an agreement with Willys

whereby they would build Jeeps under licence and commenced production of CJ3Bs which were redesignated Mitsubishi J3s. From this they developed a range of Jeep-like vehicles including steel-bodied station wagons. Nissan introduced its first 4x4 in 1948 which they named the Patrol 4W60. It was powered by a 224-cubic inch (3670-cc) six-cylinder sidevalve engine and had a wheelbase that measured 86.5 inches (220cm). The name Patrol is still used by Nissan. By the end of the fifties Toyota coined the name Land Cruiser that has endured to this day. The other large Japanese manufacturers such as Suzuki, Daihatsu and Isuzu entered the market much later.

Land Rover offered Forward Control versions of its 4x4s from 1962 until the early seventies. One example is this 1963 Series IIa model. It is owned by George and Phillip Shaw of West Yorkshire, England.

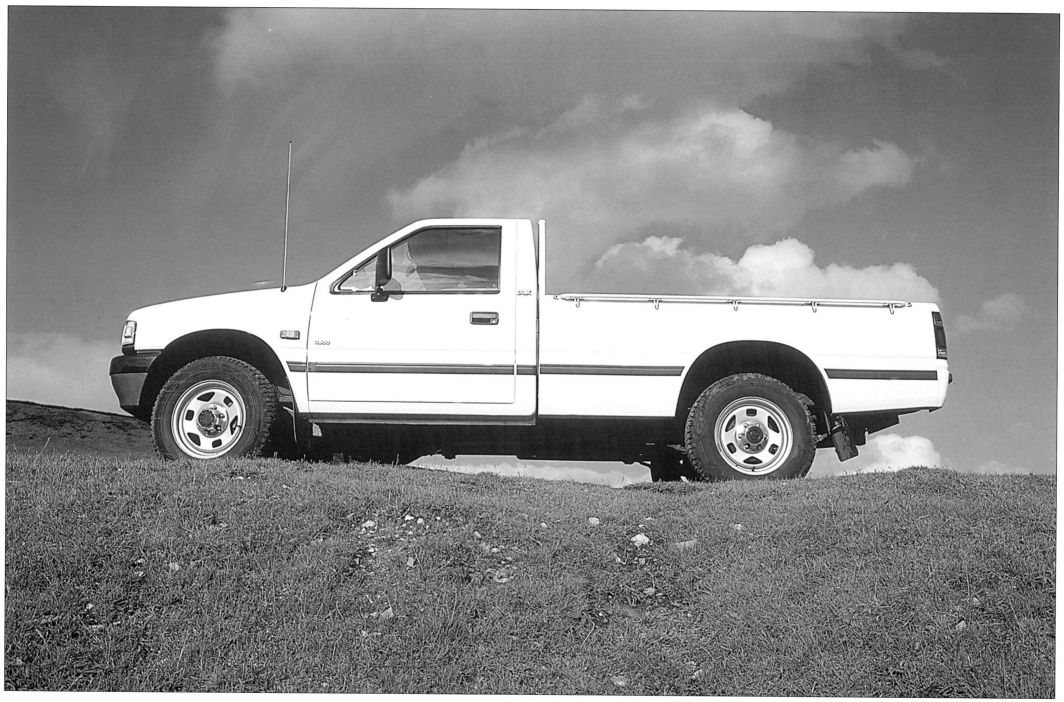

LEFT
Almost all the Japanese
manufacturers offer a four-wheel-
drive pickup truck. This Nissan 4x4 is
in use in California while the Isuzu
pickup (OPPOSITE) is sold in
England as the Vauxhall Brava.

DAIHATSU

Daihatsu of Ikeda City, Osaka, introduced the F10 'Taft' in 1974. It was a very basic off-road light truck with a 58.5-cubic inch (958-cc) four-cylinder engine and a four-speed gearbox with a two-speed transfer box. Four- and six-seat versions were available. The F20 series followed in 1977 with a choice of soft or hard tops, a choice of a 98-cubic inch (1600-cc) petrol or 154-cubic inch (2530-cc) diesel engine and a choice of short or long wheelbases. The vehicle was steel-bodied and was a completely traditional 4x4 with a wheelbase of almost 80 inches (203cm) for the short wheelbase variant. Another restyle followed in 1983 and the vehicles that sold around the world designated the F80, and known as the Rocky or Fourtrak, were announced. The F80 remained a serious and traditional machine with leaf springs and live axles. A part-time 4x4 system and four-speed transmission with high and low ratios was standard equipment along with a

choice of either a 122-cubic inch (1998-cc) petrol engine or 169-cubic inch (2765cc) diesel. A soft top variant was designated the F70 and was mechanically similar.

ISUZU

Isuzu is based in Tokyo, Japan and in 1967 introduced a two-wheel-drive field car called the Unicab KR80 which soon diversified into a true off-road vehicle of which the most well known is the 4x4 station wagon which is available in two wheelbases. Like several other manufacturers' 4x4s, it is sold and manufactured around the world under a variety of names including Trooper, Bighorn, Monterey, Passport, Jackaroo and Rodeo. There have also been commercial and truck variants and a soft top model. The 1988 model specification included independent front double-wishbone torsion bar suspension with a more traditional leaf-sprung axle at the rear. Disc brakes were fitted front and rear and the suspension was mounted to a steel ladder-frame chassis. Both diesel- and petrol-engined variants were manufactured. The vehicle was redesigned for the nineties and featured a coil sprung rear axle and a range of newer engines.

MITSUBISHI

While this Tokyo-based manufacturer continued making CJ3B Jeeps and derivatives, for its home market in particular, it launched a new 4x4 on the world market in 1981. The new machine was known by various names in different countries but Pajero and Shogun seem to have been widely used, particularly in Europe, and Montero was used in the United States. Its boxy shape was modern and both petrol- and diesel-engined variants were available. The new model was relatively traditional in that it featured a steel ladder-frame chassis and a part-time four-wheel-drive system. New technology appeared in the form of front disc brakes, independent front suspension, automatic free-wheeling hubs and a five-speed transmission.

NISSAN

In 1965 Nissan of Tokyo unveiled the 4W65 Station Wagon which looked remarkably like the Willys-Overland station wagon and had all-steel bodywork and seated eight people. It was completely conventional and used a 241-cubic inch (3956-cc) 105 bhp in-line six-cylinder engine that drove through a four-speed gearbox with high and low ratio to two leaf-sprung live axles. Soon after this followed the L60 Patrol which, although more Jeep-like in concept, had an identity all its own. It was produced throughout the sixties and early seventies and was only gradually updated and improved. There were soft top versions that featured folding windscreens and hardtop station wagons in three wheelbases. The vehicle was steel-bodied, angular and functional. The engine was a six-cylinder unit with three-speed transmission and a two-speed transfer box, all based on a welded steel box section chassis and leaf-sprung live axles. In 1980 the Patrol was relaunched in a redesigned form, once again with a choice of wheelbase lengths and roof configurations. Since then, as the popularity of trucks has exponentially increased, it has been redesigned and face-lifted yet again.

The Japanese motor manufacturers offered numerous compact pickups. Some, including Mazda, supplied its own trucks for marketing as the compact trucks of other manufacturers. The Chevy LUV was in fact a Japanese compact, for example, while Subaru marketed what could be described as a sub-compact around the world which was sold as the Subaru Brat in the United States and offered all the convenience of a 4x4.

The Toyota Hilux is probably the best known of the Japanese four-wheel-drive pickups and has been in production for almost 20 years although it has been redesigned and upgraded in this period. This particular one is used as a maintenance vehicle at a ski resort and is seen here in summer although its 4x4 system would undoubtedly be useful in winter snow when the resort is at its busiest.

SUZUKI

In April 1970, a vehicle called the Jimny 360 went on sale in Japan. It was powered by an air-cooled 22-cubic inch (359-cc) two-stroke engine. It was both traditional in terms of its transmission and suspension layouts and basic in the extreme. It was based on the Hope Star ON360 that had been developed and briefly marketed by the Hope Motor Company which was acquired by Suzuki of Hamamatsu in 1968. Australia was an early export market for the Jimny where customers were soon clamouring for similar vehicles but with larger engines and a model was marketed with a three-cylinder 34-cubic inch (550-cc)

water-cooled engine and subsequently a four- cylinder four-stroke that displaced 49 cubic inches (797cc). This latter vehicle was known as the LJ80.

In 1980 Suzuki introduced the new SJ Series that featured a redesigned chassis, new axles and a 59-cubic inch (970-cc) four-cylinder engine. It was slightly longer than the LJ and featured a redesigned chassis, new axles and a redesigned body shell. Since then, there have been any number of commercial variants including soft tops, hardtops, vans, a variety of wheelbases, licence-built models (most notably by Santana SA of Spain after 1982) and a long wheelbase closed cab pickup. Later came the

SJ413 with an 81-cubic inch (1324-cc) engine and wider track axles but was otherwise very similar.

TOYOTA LAND CRUISER

From the humble beginnings of the BJ, Toyota's four-wheel-drive vehicles progressed rapidly. The name Land Cruiser has been continuously in use by the Nagoya, Japan-based concern since it first appeared on the completely restyled version of the BJ which was referred to as the FJ-Series. These models still bore a resemblance to the Jeep with flat wings and a flat windscreen but soon evolved into Toyota's own businesslike vehicle which rapidly found favour in export markets such as Asia and Africa. As a result, the vehicles are numerous and have earned themselves a good reputation. Since the sixties there have been any number of FJ-Series variants in a number of wheelbases ranging from short wheelbase station wagons to long wheelbase pickups. More recently there have been differing Toyota truck models that still bear the Land Cruiser name being simultaneosly produced for mainly different but sometimes overlapping markets. On the whole the Toyota has remained true to the idea of leaf-sprung axles on a sturdy ladder chassis

TOYOTA HILUX

This vehicle is probably one of the all-time top-ten light trucks despite its relatively recent introduction. Recreational four-wheeling was a massively growing sport in the United States, despite the oil crisis of 1979–80, as well as the acceptance that Japanese manufacturers did offer a quality product, and this meant that when Toyota first introduced the Hilux pickup in 1979, it still found eager buyers. Prior to this there had been independent conversions of two-wheel-drive Japanese pickups into 4x4s and this had further fuelled the demands of the market. It soon became apparent that the new truck could do anything a CJ Jeep could, despite its smaller engine. The first Toyota Hiluxes were fitted with in-line four-cylinder engines of relatively small displacement but sufficient to perform well and deliver reasonable fuel economy. Off the tarmac, the truck was proving popular and recreational users began customizing their machines with roll bars and bigger wheels and tyres, suspension lift kits, winches,

and any number of other truck accessories. Suddenly, a whole new genre of off-road vehicles had arrived which were to spread beyond the United States. The other Japanese manufacturers, including Nissan, Isuzu and Mitsubishi, soon introduced 4x4 variants of their 4x2 pickups.

Mitsubishi's current model sells around the world under a variety of names including the Triton, Mighty Max and L200. Even commercials are built under licence and for a time Volkswagen built the long running Toyota Hilux pickup and sold it in Europe as a VW Taro. The Hilux has been extensively upgraded in its fifteen-year history; the body has become smoother over the years and the suspension has been upgraded from leaf springs to coils. In the United States the new generation of Toyota trucks are referred to as Tacomas and are assembled in Fremont, California.

The current range of Isuzu pickups, both two- and four-wheel-drive models seen here, are sold as Vauxhall Bravas in Britain. The two-wheel-drive model is in the foreground with the 4x4 behind it.

Chapter 9
HOT-ROD TRUCKS

*No book about pickup trucks would be complete without at least
a brief chapter on hot-rods.*

The hot-rod has its origins in thirties California when enthusiasts began to strip down cars – mostly 1932 V8 Fords – which would ultimately evolve into the multi-million dollar sport of drag racing. Hot-rods spread far beyond California and 1932 Fords and pickup trucks were soon rodded; big V8s were installed, roofs lowered or 'chopped', as it was described, suspensions lowered, and a host of other modifications made limited only by the imagination. The hot-rod truck was a natural progression from the hot-rod car, simply because so many of the light trucks shared the front end sheetmetal with the cars of the same year and favourites soon included the thirties Fords and Willys models. Pickups had the added attraction of being able to haul loads and be used as back-up trucks to race cars carrying spares and tool kits.

Trends exist within the hot-rod scene as much as anywhere else and as hot-rods became street-rods so too did the rodded trucks. The resto-rod fashion of the seventies – building a street-rod that appeared at a glance to be a restored stock car – was suited to trucks as well as cars and trends exclusive to trucks

soon appeared. Alongside the resto-rod 1932 Fords and 1941 Willys trucks another trend of the early seventies began to emerge, that of people who were into trucks – pickups and vans – and wished to customize, rod them, or simply improve them for whatever purpose interested them, be it off-roading, drag racing or whatever. Vans were treated to bold custom paint jobs covering large expanses of sheetmetal and there were wild custom interiors, while classic pickups such as 1955 Chevrolets were lowered, fitted with bigger V8s and painted in startling colours. Unlike the street-rod scene, where it had to be a pre-1948 vehicle to be a real rod, the truck scene welcomed all-comers in everything from new Japanese compacts to full-size classics. Mini-trucks soon became a popular subsection, simply because they were affordable and plentiful, and paint jobs encompassed modern graphics and classic flames fanning upwards. Street-rod techniques – such as installing Jaguar IRS (independent rear suspension) under a truck – became popular in conjunction with engine swaps. By 1977 three main strands had merged, vanning, classic trucking and modern trucking. Flames crossed all

Larry Sterkel's 1935 Ford pickup street-rod. This rod was built from scratch using the vintage Ford truck and chassis but with the installation of a Heidt front-end kit to fit Mustang parts, a Maverick rear axle and a 302 Ford V8. The truck rolls on Budnik alloy wheels and is finished in Porsche Red.

boundaries as a popular choice of paint scheme while massive murals were on the whole reserved for the sides of vans such as Ford's Econoline. Roof chops were another street-rod and custom car technique applied to both vans and trucks. Big events began to establish themselves such as the massive gathering for classic F-100 owners, the Reno F-100 run. The off-road and 4x4 scene got bigger towards the end of the seventies, increasing interest in desert racing, and introduced a new style to the truck scene, the

off-road look. This included off-road tyres, pre-runner bumpers, lift kits and more. The eighties saw a resurgence of interest in custom vans and mushrooming interest in vintage and classic trucks, whether stock or heavily modified. The mini-truck scene began to get more sophisticated as cabriolet conversions and similar became commonplace. They also began to feature European sportscar styling and components. On the other hand, four-wheel-drive trucks were often fitted with suspension lift kits

ABOVE AND RIGHT Carol Smith's 1930 Model A Ford street-rod. The rod is powered by a 327-cubic inch (5359cc) V8, has a Mustang rear axle, a lowered I-beam front axle and Western wheels. The truck cab has been modified and the load bed shortened. It is seen here in Fort Collins, Colorado.

OPPOSITE Tim Walters built this 1954 Chevrolet pickup in Denver, Colorado. The truck is now powered by a 350 Chevrolet V8 and has 1974 Camaro suspension set up at the front and a Camaro rear axle at the rear. The wheels are from a Corvette and the truck is finished in two shades of green. It took six years to build from an $800 beater.

and massive off-road tyres on custom wheels to boost their performance in events where the going was sticky and to allow them to scale larger obstacles off-road. The mid-eighties also saw the emergence of the massive monster show truck, off-roaders on massive wheels and tyres with multiple shock-absorber set-up and wild finishes.

The mid-eighties also saw the rise of specific names being given to different types of truck; early trucks were called haulers, fast early trucks remained truck-rods, compacts (either U.S.-made or imported) were referred to simply as minis and custom half-tons were known as sport trucks. As the decade progressed, new events such as truck racing on race tracks became popular and, like desert racing, attracted sponsorship from both truck and component manufacturers.

The nineties saw the mini-trucking and classic scenes booming in popularity and diverging to some degree. The classic scene remained traditional while the minis continued to get more outrageous with ever-larger stereo systems and wilder graphic paint jobs, the pro-street, drag-strip look proving popular for

trucks. Classic haulers continued to be popular with some building street-rod haulers from old COE – cab-over-engine – trucks on modern chassis. The race track series of truck racing became a NASCAR series and attracted top-name drivers to the multi-round NASCAR championship at venues that included Watkins Glen, Indianapolis, Sears Point and Phoenix International raceway. (NASCAR is the sanctioning body of American stock-car racing.)

Some of the most spectacular events are the off-road races: in North America there are a series of desert races run under the auspices of SCORE (Southern California Off Road Enterprises) and the HDRA (High Desert Racing Association) of which the two most famous are the Mint 400 and the Baja 1000. The number suffix is an indication of the race's length in miles while the name is relevant to its location, the Baja 1000 being run on the Baja peninsula in Mexico while the Mint 400 is based in Las Vegas, the Mint being a casino that was once a major sponsor. However, that race is now called the Nissan 400 due to a change of sponsorship. The Baja 1000 has been running for more than 25 years and is renowned for its toughness, as is the Nissan 400.

Street-rods, such as the GMC (OPPOSITE) and this Chevrolet (LEFT) photographed at Southfork Ranch in Dallas, Texas, are finished to such a high standard that it is hard to imagine that they were ever working trucks.

Other American desert races include the Fireworks 250, the Las Vegas 250 and the Parker 400. There are fiercely contended classes for almost every type of pickup truck, 4x4 as well as off-road buggy. Some classes attract huge professional teams sponsored by manufacturers and importers of 4x4s as success in off-road racing can result in increased sales. In recent years both Ford, Chevrolet and Toyota have made strong showings in the truck classes while Jeep Cherokee racers have gained honours in the Pro/Stock Mini-truck class. Other extensive sponsorship comes from parts and accessories manufacturers such as tyre companies which include BF Goodrich and Yokohama who see off-road racing as an ideal test-bed for their products. Manufacturers of shock-absorbers as well as oil companies also support off-road racing, having a professional interest in good results.

These two heavily modified Fords, one from the forties (OPPOSITE), the other from the fifties (BELOW) illustrate how successfully varying body-styles lend themselves to the custom treatment. The 1940 Ford features a flame-effect paint job, which is a perennial favourite of hot-rodders, while the pastel finish of the other is the more classic choice.

OVERLEAF
Ole Yeller is a hybrid, constructed from the body of a 1956 Chevrolet pickup and the chassis and running gear of a 1979 4x4 Chevrolet Blazer.

PAGE 111
Another modified fifties Chevrolet pickup is this customized version on display in an indoor rod and custom show.

INDEX